BEHAVE YOURSELF!
The essential guide to international etiquette

Michael Powell

INSIDERS' GUIDE®

Published in North America by The Globe Pequot Press
Copyright © JW Cappelens forlag under licence from Gusto Company AS
www.gusto.tv
Written by Michael Powell
Original concept by Michael Powell, James Tavendale and Ernesto Gremese
Edited by Katherine Robinson

Cover design and illustration: Melkeveien Designkontor, www.melkeveien.no
Text design: Melkeveien Designkontor, www.melkeveien.no
Photo credits: Getty Images

Library of Congress Cataloging-in-Publication Data is available

ISBN - 10: 0-7627-3672-0
ISBN - 13: 978-0-7627-3672-0

Printed and Manufactured in Italy
First Edition/Fifth Printing

Table of Contents

BEHAVE YOURSELF!
The essential guide to international etiquette

Introduction

"The gentle reader will never, never know what consummate ass he can become, until he goes abroad."

—Mark Twain

Navigating the treacherous waters of international etiquette has never been easy. Most of us spring a leak at some point during our travels around strange and exotic lands; some of us run aground on the craggy headlands of our own inflexibility; others float rudderless in a sea of cultural ambivalence; an unlucky few catch a dose of bilharzia and have their credit cards stolen within 10 minutes of stepping ashore.

So what is the secret of savvy traveling? What separates the ignorant tourist from the streetwise explorer, the walking ATM machine from the attentive haggler, the genteel jet-setter from the diplomatic dunderhead? Just one thing:

NEVER FORGET THAT YOU ARE THE FOREIGNER.

Of course, it also helps to keep an open mind and a sense of humor, to have a positive regard for others, and to always flush the toilet (especially in Singapore).

Trying to highlight national characteristics can feel a bit simplistic, but it is a fact that manners and correct behavior are learned; we aren't born with them. What is polite in some cultures may be downright insulting in others. How can you behave yourself if you don't know how to behave?

Whenever you go abroad, I hope you will use this book as your personal flotation device. Not literally, since this edition is printed on mere paper and provides minimal buoyancy—however, it will give you essential traveling tips, such as how to greet and say goodbye; what to wear; how and what to eat; what to talk about; when to show up late and when to be on time; where yes or a nod of the head means no; and how to avoid being arrested for jaywalking, chewing gum, or taking a nap in your car.

Don't risk leaving home without a copy. In fact, pack two—it's always good to have a backup, and who knows, during a prolonged bout of dysentery in a Marrakech *khazi*, it could prove doubly handy. . . .

DISCLAIMER: Information about medical precautions (such as inoculations) and whether the countries included within these pages are safe to visit is not included in this book, as it is subject to change. If in doubt, always check with your embassy before traveling.

Argentina

Meeting and Greeting

If you are meeting someone for the first time, you should shake hands, but thereafter, Argentineans may use the customary kiss on the right cheek. Both men and women greet each other in this way. Kiss or shake hands again upon departure.

Personal space is small. Argentineans stand close, so don't back away; they will think you are being shy and quickly close the gap again. Or, worse, they will think you are being unfriendly.

Conversation

While the national language is Spanish, the dominant dialect spoken is Castilian, which is heavily influenced by Italian.

If you're stuck for conversation (which is unlikely, because Argentineans are very friendly), talk about *futbol* or *tango*—the two national obsessions. Discussing politics is also popular, but avoid talking about Brazil, Argentina's archrival.

Eating and Drinking

Restaurants open very late, rarely earlier than 8 p.m., so resign yourself to not being able to get a meal much earlier than this. Most people arrive around 9 p.m.

he most popular drink is *mate*, a sort of tea made by pouring hot water on the crushed leaves of the *yerba mate* (a kind of pumpkin). It s drunk *dulce* (with sugar) or *amargo* (without ugar) from a special wooden gourd-like eceptacle with a metal spout.

Keep your knife and fork in your right and left hands, respectively, at all times; don't put down our knife to eat with your fork in the United States style. Keep your hands visible on top of he table, but don't put your elbows on the table.

During meals, Argentineans usually dilute their vine with soda water. Pour wine with your right hand; pouring with the left hand is considered uncouth.

Out and About

f you think a bird has done its business on your shoulder, you may be the victim of pickpockets. Their ploy is to throw mustard at unsuspecting victims, and then make a big show of coming to the person's aid and helping them clean off the mess, when actually they are stealing their belongings. If anyone tries to help you clean bird droppings off of your clothes, stay away from that person.

A common gesture is to rock the right hand a few times, palm facing upward, while keeping the fingers together at an angle. This gesture means anything from "What's going on?" to "I don't understand" to "Wicked!"

Maintain good posture—no slouching or relaxed poses. Do not put your hands in your pockets.

Do not yawn or stretch in public. All of these are perceived as rude.

When changing currency or receiving change, check to make sure you are being given pesos. After the economic crisis of 2001, a local currency called *lecops* or *patacones* was issued with limited circulation, and few places will accept it. These notes are easy to distinguish from pesos because they have no picture on the back, only writing. Don't accept this currency from anyone.

Dress
Wear lightweight, quality clothes. A suit should be dark, and ties should be well made and conservative. Women should aim for simple elegance with a minimum of makeup.

Gifts and Tips
When visiting an Argentinean home, always arrive with a gift of flowers or candy and something for any children present.

In business, women should not give gifts to male colleagues; the gesture might be misinterpreted as a proposition. Always open gifts immediately.

Restaurants often include a 10 percent service charge, but it is customary to add another 10 percent for good service.

Australia

Meeting and Greeting

Greet with a firm handshake while maintaining good eye contact. Australians may say "G'day, mate" regardless of your gender, but you shouldn't wear out the greeting. It can sit uncomfortably and appear a little patronizing coming from a foreigner.

Punctuality is quite relaxed—but don't push it!

Conversation

Australians are friendly, open, and relaxed. Above all, they dislike anyone who thinks he or she is better than someone else. This is called the *tall poppy syndrome*, referring to the way poppies growing taller than their surroundings tend to get picked first. Australian society is fiercely egalitarian, and any attempt to pull rank or show off your status will be challenged or knocked down with sarcastic humor.

Australians have strong opinions and enjoy being provocative and direct, but they generally don't take themselves too seriously. An ability to laugh at yourself or take a joke at your expense is very useful here.

Don't bring up the subject of convicts or *Crocodile Dundee*. Australians are tired of the comparisons, and it will make you look like a *galah* (a stupid native bird). Also, don't confuse Australians with Kiwis (New Zealanders). They are as different as Canadians and Americans.

Eating and Drinking

Australians enjoy a good drinking session, and everyone is expected to pay for a *shout* (round of drinks).

When dining out, expect to pay for your share unless you have been specifically invited out for a special treat at your host's expense.

Don't stand on ceremony at a barbecue. Your hosts will expect you to get "stuck in" and enjoy yourself without asking for permission at every step. Serve yourself and make yourself at home.

Eating, drinking, or smoking are not permitted in public buildings, shops, or public transportation.

Out and About
Don't arrive unannounced at someone's house. Arrange a visit beforehand.

Personal space is large. Maintain at least an arm's length of distance between you and someone else.

Australian men aren't big on hugging, touching, or other friendly expressions of physical contact. If you consider yourself a sensitive man, then spare the feelings and embarrassment of others and take your lead from your hosts.

When riding in a taxi, it is polite to sit in the front seat—another expression of the egalitarian Aussie spirit. Don't hitchhike; it will make you vulnerable and mark you as a tourist.

Don't use the thumbs-up sign. It means "up yours."

Dress
Business dress is quite conservative, although it may be more relaxed in tropical areas. Take your lead from those around you.

Even though the culture is laid back and the climate is hot, this does not give you license to lose your sense of modesty. Women should be especially sensitive in the more rural areas, where traditional values dominate.

Gifts and Tips
In business, gift-giving is rare, but you should bring a small token when invited to someone's home—a bottle of wine, flowers, or chocolates.

Tipping in restaurants is not the norm, but you may add 10 percent to the bill if you have received excellent service. Likewise, you might tip a couple of dollars to taxi drivers, waiters, and hotel porters, but all tipping is optional and not expected.

Austria

become more familiar, and handshakes may be replaced by air kisses on both cheeks.

Upon leaving, another handshake is customary, accompanied by "Auf Wiedersehen" or "Auf Wiederschauen," which both mean "until we see each other again."

Conversation

Austrians, perhaps more so than other nationalities, greatly appreciate a little knowledge of their unique culture and history. To lump them together with Germans will cause offense. They are very different, especially in their language.

Austrians are very well-behaved and are sticklers for doing things the right way and obeying the rules. But they are also very direct and will take what you say very literally, so idle promises or invitations, such as "We must do this again sometime," will be taken at face value.

Eating and Drinking

Along with an Austrian's sense of decorum comes his *Gemütlichkeit*, or appreciation of the finer things in life—including good food and drink enjoyed in agreeable company. (The drinking age is 16.) Eating heartily and displaying your appetite and love of food are encouraged. Try a little or a lot of everything that is offered; otherwise, you may offend your host by seeming to reject his or her hospitality.

Meeting and Greeting

Austrians are very polite and quite formal—some would say uptight—based on a genuine belief in showing respect to others, observing the correct protocol, and being courteous at all times. Being punctual is very important.

Shake hands with everyone in the room (even children), maintain eye contact, and say "Grüß Gott" ("God's greeting"). Wait for a woman to offer her hand for a handshake.

When entering a shop or restaurant, you should acknowledge everyone with a "Grüß Gott." When walking down the street you will be greeted in the same way, to which you should reply, "Grüß Gott" or "Grüß dich" (a more informal "Hello") if the person greeting you is a child. You should initiate the greeting when the other person is older than you. If you are greeted by someone you know, reply "Servus" ("Your servant"—equivalent to "at your service").

The first few meetings will be quite formal and polite, but the interaction will relax after you

Don't start eating until your host has wished you "Guten Appetit" or "Mahlzeit" (two variations meaning "Bon Appetit") and has started to eat.

Keep your hands visible on top of the table, but do not put your elbows on the table.

Cut your food with your fork. Using a knife suggests that the food is tough.

When toasting someone, always look the person in the eye and say "Prost" (something like "Cheers"). Austrians view toasting as an opportunity to acknowledge others and really connect with them, so clinking or raising a glass without making eye contact is not just an empty gesture, it is also the height of rudeness.

In a restaurant or bar, never sit at a table labeled *Stammtisch*, which means it is reserved for the regulars.

Out and About
Smoking is not allowed in many public places, although there are smoking sections in restaurants.

Austrian politeness may result in drivers stopping to allow pedestrians to cross the road, even when there's lots of traffic.

When staying in an Austrian's home, be aware that water is metered and is expensive, so don't waste it, and avoid taking long showers.

Divide your trash into five different categories for recycling; otherwise, you may incur a fine.

Austrian formality means that placing hands in your pockets will not be interpreted as being laid back; rather, it will make you appear socially awkward, lacking in confidence, and even rude.

Dress
Austrians are smart dressers who believe in presenting a clean and elegant image. The emphasis is on high-quality, conservative, well-made clothing, not ostentatious designer labels and jewelry.

Remove your shoes when visiting an Austrian home. Many women bring their own slippers that coordinate with their outfit, as it is more dignified than wandering around in socks or nylons.

Gifts and Tips
There isn't a culture of gift-giving in business circles, but if you are given a gift, you should open it immediately and show your appreciation. When you are invited to an Austrian home, always take a good-quality gift or an odd number of flowers, since an odd number is considered lucky (avoid roses, which are too personal, and chrysanthemums, which are associated with funerals).

In restaurants, a tip of up to 10 percent is acceptable and expected, or round off the bill to the nearest 50 or 100 schillings.

Belgium

Conversation

Belgium is composed of three linguistic groups and 10 provinces. The north (Flanders) is Flemish (Dutch)-speaking; the south (Wallonia) is French-speaking; and there is also a small German-speaking enclave in the east. Always be aware of whom you are addressing and to which group they belong. However, don't highlight this linguistic and cultural diversity, as it can be an uneasy subject. Remember, Belgium has repeatedly been occupied by foreign powers.

The Belgians are not demonstrably patriotic, and their culture is very diverse and often difficult for an outsider to define in simple terms. If you are tempted to dismiss them as parochial and lacking in a national identity, keep quiet and try to open yourself to the subtleties of this highly individualistic and pragmatic society.

Belgians appear reserved and starchy at first, but they have a subtle and self-deprecating sense of humor. Boasting or showing off your status is not welcome here, as the natives are egalitarian and antiauthoritarian, despite their apparent formality. They are also very tolerant of other cultures and they dislike moralizing, so if you've got strong opinions, keep them to yourself. Live and let live.

Belgians' subversive nature is demonstrated by the affection they hold for one of their most popular, if understated, tourist attractions—the *Manneken Pis* in Brussels—a tiny statue of a little boy urinating into a fountain.

Meeting and Greeting

Shake hands when greeting and departing. Greet every member of a group individually with a handshake.

Stand up when greeting a woman, and wait for her to offer her hand.

Belgians reserve *les trois bises* (three air cheek kisses, alternating right, left, right) for those they know well. Don't presume to initiate this greeting, but be prepared to reciprocate if someone offers his or her cheek.

14

Use *Monsieur, Madame,* or *Mademoiselle* for French-speakers, or *Meneer, Mevrouw,* or *Juffrouw* for Flemish-speakers, to mean Mr., Mrs., or Miss.

Speak in a calm and composed manner at all times. Raising your voice, gesturing, or becoming too animated is unwelcome.

Maintain good posture—no slouching or hanging loose. Do not put your hands in your pockets.

Eating and Drinking

When toasting, raise your glass twice—once while the toast is being said and again just before drinking.

It is polite to eat everything on your plate and enjoy your food. The Belgians relish the good life, and they don't like to be wasteful. Compliment the food. Belgians take their cuisine very seriously, and it sets a very high standard.

Smoking is widespread and allowed in most places. Offer your cigarettes around before lighting up. Don't smoke during a meal, although it is acceptable to do so before the food arrives and after the dessert has been cleared away.

The penalty for drunk driving is severe and may result in a prison sentence.

Out and About

Belgians are not comfortable with a lot of bodily contact, so maintain an arm's length of personal space and avoid backslapping and other overt physical expressions.

Don't drop into a Belgian home unannounced—even family members phone first to make arrangements to visit.

Use your whole hand when pointing, and don't chew gum or blow your nose in public.

Dress

In keeping with their dignity and sense of decorum, Belgians dress well and judge others on their personal appearance. Good-quality clothes and simple elegance are respected.

Gifts and Tips

Gift-giving is rare in business circles, but you should bring flowers or wine when visiting a Belgian home. Don't bother bringing chocolates from home, since they make some of the best in the world. Open gifts immediately and show your appreciation with quiet dignity.

Restaurant bills include 15 percent service charge and value-added tax (VAT), but you may leave an extra tip for excellent service.

Brazil

Meeting and Greeting

Being punctual is not a priority. Arriving even 15 minutes late will not be considered a serious breach of etiquette. Sometimes lateness can feel like the national pastime.

When business relationships are formed, you are in there for the long haul. You will be expected to show loyalty and commitment rather than taking the money and running. Business is usually done face to face rather than over the phone or by e-mail, and it usually takes many appointments to broker a deal.

Brazilians touch a lot, and personal space is very small. A first meeting will involve a handshake with sustained eye contact, but once you become more familiar, you may receive a quick hug and a back slap from a man, while women exchange air kisses to each cheek between one and four times while shaking hands. Married women more commonly use two kisses; single women generally use three.

Say "Oi" for "Hi" and "Ciao" for "Bye."

In business circles, shake hands with everyone in the group upon departure.

Conversation

The national language is Portuguese. Don't speak Spanish unless you want to offend someone.

Conversations may get quite loud and animated with much gesturing. Expect a lot of noise at restaurants, cinemas, and theaters. Be yourself and talk in your normal voice; don't feel like you have to increase the volume and tempo to fit in, although if you do raise your voice, it isn't a problem. But always maintain good eye contact.

If you're stuck for conversation (which is unlikely, because the Brazilians are so gregarious and friendly), talk about *futebol*, the national obsession. Avoid talking about politics or Brazil's archrival, Argentina.

Don't be surprised if you receive an invitation to the home of an acquaintance.

Brazilians are very optimistic and believe that it is possible to find a solution to any problem. This is called Brazilian *jeito*; sometimes it refers to bribery, but often it expresses a positive outlook that there is always a way.

Eating and Drinking

Always use a knife and fork, even for finger foods, including sandwiches, fruit, and pizza.

Brazilians tend to eat with the fork, while the knife sits with the blade resting on the plate and the handle on the table when it is not being used.

Keep your elbows off the table.

Smoking is not allowed in many public places.

Don't eat in public places or on the street. Brazilians don't like eating on the go. They prefer to eat slowly, so meals usually last a long time. Brazilians take their families out to dinner at all hours (dinner starts late), and children are common in restaurants in the evening.

Out and About

Expect a lot of physical contact—hugs, backslaps, and arm-touching.

Yawning or stretching in public is rude.

If someone flicks his fingers underneath his chin, it means "I don't know" or "I don't

understand." Don't use the OK hand gesture, which is considered a rude gesture with obscene connotations.

Brazilians begin socializing late in the evening, with many people not going out until 11 p.m. Dinner parties may easily last to 2 a.m. and beyond. If you're invited to a party, it will usually be at a club rather than at someone's home. Arrive about 15 minutes late.

Dress

Wear lightweight, quality clothes. A suit should be dark, and ties should be well-made and conservative. Women should aim for simple elegance with a minimal amount of makeup.

Gifts and Tips

Make sure that gifts aren't black or purple; these are colors of mourning. Avoid sharp gifts, such as letter openers, scissors, or knives, which mean you wish to end a relationship. Small electronic items are more popular than wallets, perfume, or jewelry.

Many restaurants add a 10 percent service charge. Add another five percent for good service.

Bulgaria

Meeting and Greeting

The most common greeting is a firm handshake while maintaining good eye contact. Shaking hands again upon departure is optional.

Conversation

Bulgarians tend to downplay their achievements and dislike those who try too hard or show off (about wealth, for example). Even if you are making minimum wage at home, you are still earning three times as much as they are. Be sensitive to the fact that relations between Turkey and Bulgaria are strained. (A common theme in Bulgarian art and folk music is the centuries-long struggle against Ottoman oppression.)

Eating and Drinking

Lunch is the main meal of the day. Dinner is a social event, and dancing is common in many restaurants.

Out and About

Bulgarians, especially the older generation, shake their heads to say "yes" and nod to say "no."

Be sure that you are given a *carte statistique*, or border control card, by Customs officials upon arrival in the country; you cannot check into a hotel without it.

Avoid using travelers' checks; few places will cash them. Change currency on the border (and keep your *bordereaux* receipt, which indicates the amount of currency exchanged, until you leave). ATM machines are available in Sofia and a few other places, but don't pull out too much cash because you can't take it out of the country. Never change money on the street—you will either be conned or given worthless, obsolete notes.

It is illegal to take antiques out of the country, and besides, they are probably fakes or stolen.

Watch out for fake police, who drive around at night in ordinary cars with blue lights and ask for your papers and money. Genuine police patrol in the daytime as well and have official cars. If you suspect that you have been stopped by a fake policeman, insist on accompanying him to the police station on foot; do not climb into his car.

Speed limits are strictly enforced, and traffic police are everywhere. They will stop you (by holding up a handheld stop sign) even if you are going only slightly over the limit. For a first offense, you will probably receive a warning, but subsequent offenses will result in your passport being stamped. If this happens, you will have to pay a fine when you leave.

The Mafia controls most of the business; these people are easy to spot because they have expensive clothes and cars. Stay away from them.

Dress

Dress smartly, with simple elegance, in well-made clothes, but avoid clothing that makes you stand out or broadcasts your wealth. Expect to see well-dressed citizens (not just Mafia members) in Sofia, which is one of the most chic cities of the former Eastern Bloc.

Remove your shoes when you enter someone's home.

Gifts and Tips

In a restaurant, the tip is not included in the bill, so add 10 percent. It is rude to place the tip into someone's hand; leave it on the table. You may find that the waiter chases you outside to tell you that you have paid too much, despite your insistence that it is supposed to be a gratuity.

Canada

Meeting and Greeting

Canada is a bilingual country, with two official languages—English and French—although most citizens are not bilingual. The province of Quebec is mainly French-speaking, and the rest of Canada is mainly English-speaking, with the exception of the province of New Brunswick, which is very mixed. Government departments must produce information in both languages, so expect to see English and French signs in airports and other municipal places.

In business, greet with a firm handshake and maintain good eye contact. In more casual circumstances, it is okay to say "Hi" and raise your hand. Canadians are generally more etiquette-conscious than Americans, and often shake hands. In Quebec, the continental cheek-kissing is popular among French-speakers.

Punctuality is important, except for a social event, when you should show up about 30 minutes late to give the host more time to prepare.

Conversation

Do not confuse Canadians with Americans; the countries have very different histories, people, and ways of life. Canadians are more reserved and cautious than Americans. The pace of life is more sedate, and tolerance of others, social welfare, and equality are more important than individualism in Canada. Competitive behavior is acceptable, but not boasting or ostentation. Speak in a calm and composed manner at all times, even though French-Canadians tend to be more animated.

Canadians use the term "people of the First Nation" versus "Native Americans," which they find offensive.

Eating and Drinking
You will find both the American and the continental use of cutlery. The fork is either held in the right hand and switched to the left or put down when the knife is used for cutting or spreading; or else the knife and fork remain in right and left hands, respectively. Both practices are acceptable.

It is polite to offer dishes around before serving yourself. Refusing food is acceptable and will not cause offense.

Don't eat food on the move. If you buy take-out food, stand or sit down to eat.

Out and About
Maintain at least an arm's length of personal space and avoid bodily contact, such as back-slapping and other overt physical expressions.

Many Americans wrongly believe that you can cross the border into Canada without any form of identification. In fact, crossing the border requires a passport, a birth certificate, or a social security card. A driver's license is not sufficient.

Placing your hands in your pockets while you are talking is considered rude. Blowing your nose into a handkerchief or tissue is acceptable as long as it is done discreetly.

Pedestrians and bicycles have the right-of-way on Canadian roads.

Dress
Business dress is slightly less formal than in the United States, but it is dressier in the evening. The emphasis is on good-quality clothing, especially shoes, rather than trendy designer labels. However, outside of business, casual clothes such as T-shirts, jeans, sweat-pants, and shorts are acceptable.

Always remove your shoes when visiting someone's house.

Gifts and Tips
Bring a small gift such as flowers or chocolates when you are visiting a Canadian home. Open any gifts you receive immediately and express your appreciation.

Restaurants include a Goods and Services Tax of seven percent in the bill, but tipping an extra 15 to 20 percent is almost obligatory. (In some bars, even if you buy one drink, you are expected to tip.) However, this depends on the quality of the establishment and the level of service. Don't be pressured into tipping unless you feel it is deserved.

Chile

Meeting and Greeting

Initial greetings are quite formal, with handshakes and direct eye contact. Although Chileans have an initial reserve that is more characteristic of Europe than Latin America, they will warm to you quickly. Greet the most senior person first, as elders are treated with great respect. Close male friends may hug and backslap briefly (the Spanish *abrazo*), while women usually air kiss each other once on the right cheek. Kiss or shake hands again upon departure.

Personal space is small. Chileans stand close, so don't back away; they will think you are being shy and quickly close the gap again. Or, worse, they will think you are being unfriendly.

Conversation

When saying goodbye, a Chilean acquaintance may say, "I'll call you later." This is just an expression, so don't sit around waiting for the phone to ring!

It is acceptable to interrupt others while they are speaking; in fact, if someone interrupts you it is a sign that they are interested and engaged in what you are saying.

Chileans are honest and trustworthy, but their politeness often leads them to give a diplomatic answer instead of the plain truth.

Eating and Drinking
Keep your knife and fork in your right and left hands, respectively, at all times; don't put down your knife to eat with your fork in the United States style. Keep your hands visible on top of the table, but not your elbows. Accept what you are given and wait to be offered seconds; don't ask for more.

When toasting someone, look that person in the eye and say "Salud." Pour wine with your right hand.

Always arrive late to a social function (unless it's an official function). Arrive at least 15 minutes late to a dinner party.

The host always pays the bill in a restaurant, and the bill arrives only after it has been requested. Women never pay; any attempt to do so may embarrass the host.

When smoking, always offer a cigarette to everyone present.

Out and About
In some South American countries bribing

police is commonplace, but in Chile it will land you in serious trouble. Do not hesitate to approach the police for assistance; they are helpful and trustworthy.

Maintain good posture—no slouching or relaxed poses. Do not put your hands in your pockets. Stand when a woman enters the room. Do not yawn or stretch in public.

Dress
Present a clean and elegant image. Chileans dress with style and sophistication; women should dress modestly and avoid showy jewelry or anything revealing or provocative. Despite their sartorial elegance, Chileans don't dress for dinner.

Gifts and Tips
When visiting a Chilean home, always arrive with a gift of flowers or candy, as well as something for any children present.

In business, women should not give gifts to male colleagues; the gesture might be misinterpreted as a proposition. Always open gifts immediately.

Restaurants often include a 10 percent service charge, but it is customary to add another 10 percent for good service.

China

Meeting and Greeting

A greeting rarely includes a handshake. The Chinese bow or nod their heads, often without a smile, as greeting is a solemn, respectful affair. If you do shake hands, do not expect to receive a firm handshake.

Punctuality is very important, especially in business. If you are with a group, arrive together.

Offer a business card with both hands and with the text facing away from you. When receiving a business card, it is polite to scrutinize it closely and then keep holding the card, rather than stuffing it into your pocket (which is rude and also signifies the end of the meeting).

A common greeting is "Have you eaten?," which is the equivalent of "How are you?" Always answer yes even if it's not true.

Conversation

If someone doesn't understand what you are saying, you may be met with a silent smile.

Keep gestures to a minimum. The Chinese use very few gestures when speaking and may find them distracting and irritating.

Saying no is hard for a Chinese person, who will prefer to say something like "perhaps" or "I'll think about it" in order to be polite. Expect to be let down very gently, since the Chinese are very diplomatic and will go out of their way to save face. If you need to discuss a sensitive subject, do so in private so you don't show someone up in public. Causing someone to lose face would be a disaster not only for your relationship, but for that person's whole family.

Eating and Drinking

Meals usually take place in restaurants rather than in private houses. Guests are usually seated according to rank, with the guests of honor seated to the right of the host. Do not start eating until the host has served the principal guest. Don't talk business during a meal.

Alcohol is practically obligatory, and your host will view it as his duty to get you drunk. Don't try to drink your Chinese hosts under the table; your desire to avoid losing face will never be as great as theirs.

Expect much toasting. The host utters the first toast with the words "Gan bei," which means

"dry the glass," after which everyone should drain their glasses. Try to maintain eye contact while drinking a toast.

Only pour yourself a drink after you have first topped off the glasses of those around you. It is polite to fill a glass as full as possible without actually spilling any liquid, as a sign of generosity and companionship.

Use the thick end of your chopsticks when taking food from a communal dish. Refusing food or drink is impolite, but don't dig around in a bowl looking for the best bits of food. Finish your rice or noodles as a sign of respect for the person who prepared the food, but leave a small amount of other food untouched to indicate that you are satisfied.

Eat rice by holding the bowl close to your face and scooping it into your mouth with your chopsticks. Leaving the bowl on the table is a sign that you are unhappy with the food. Never leave your chopsticks stuck in your rice; this is associated with death.

Slurping noodles or soup is an acceptable way of cooling it down.

Many restaurants will invite you to choose your own food, especially seafood, which is culled on the spot to ensure freshness.

Out and About
Haggle for everything. You will stand out as a tourist, so the starting price for anything will inevitably be high.

Spitting is a national obsession, although the Chinese government recently banned it to curb the spread of severe acute respiratory syndrome (SARS). Chinese people often spit for good luck, especially when they see foreigners. The roots of this tradition lie in the ancient belief that demons reside and breed in mucus, so don't be surprised if you encounter lots of people purging their throats in your direction.

The concept of standing in line is not popular in China except in banks and airports; usually, it is a free-for-all with much pushing and shoving.

Carry a supply of tissues. Bathroom facilities in all but the best hotels are very basic—usually a hole in the ground with coarse toilet paper and even stalls without doors.

As a foreigner you will attract a lot of friendly curiosity and may actually draw crowds if you stand still for too long! If you are blonde, people will wish to touch your hair continually. Take it as a compliment.

Rickshaws and bicycles do not stop at traffic lights, so watch out when you're crossing the road.

Dress
Wear smart, casual clothes, but nothing too revealing.

Gifts and Tips
Chinese people will politely decline a gift three times before accepting it. They will not open it in front of you, and nor should you.

Foreign cigarettes, wine, and spirits make good presents, but don't give flowers, white objects, or clocks, which all are associated with death.

Tipping is officially illegal, although it does happen. Often an offered tip will be politely refused and may cause embarrassment.

Croatia

Meeting and Greeting

A common greeting is "Zdravo" ("Hello") or "Bog" ("God"—used to say "Hi" and "Bye"). Shake hands firmly and maintain good eye contact; good friends may kiss and hug. Croatians are very down to earth; as long as you are open and straightforward, you will soon feel at home.

Conversation

Do not ever refer to Croatia as Yugoslavia. What do you think the war of independence was for? Don't bring up the subject of the war; almost everyone has been directly affected, and the psychological scars run deep. If it does come up, don't refer to the conflict as a civil war, since it was a reaction against Yugoslav army aggression.

If someone offers you something to eat, it is impolite to say "No, thank you." Instead, you should say "I cannot" ("Ne mogu.") The safest option is never to refuse food, which can be difficult because you will be offered it nonstop!

Don't talk about your lifestyle back home unless you are invited to do so, and then do not make a big deal of it. You will impress no one with your boasting. Even if you are working for minimum wage, you still will be earning three times as much as the Croatians. Expect to be asked how much you earn, and be prepared to say something tactful, such as "enough." Always strive to be down to earth.

Eating and Drinking

Croatian hospitality is considerable, and you will therefore be offered plate after plate of food and lots to drink. Always accept someone's hospitality, and try to sample a little of everything, since the hostess invariably will have spent the whole day preparing the meal. Your wine glass will be topped off endlessly unless you leave it half full.

Don't eat at a restaurant if you are in a hurry. You will be served slowly, making it a long process to enjoy your meal. You'll find that having you pay the bill seems low on the restaurateur's list of priorities.

Out and About

Croatia is now one of the safest countries in the world. Crime is almost nonexistent, and it is common to see young children walking home alone after dark. A local joke claims that corruption and crime are only committed by politicians.

Haggling in markets and tourist shops is acceptable. Croatia has a long history of tourism, so the people are experts at spotting a gullible foreigner ready to part with his money.

By law you must register with the local authorities within 48 hours of arrival in a town. If you are staying in a hotel, you usually will be asked to leave your passport at reception for a day, and they will sort out this procedure for you. If you are staying with friends, you must visit the police station yourself. You will receive a registration card that gives your address and date of arrival, which you should carry at all times along with your passport.

One of the legacies of the war is the danger of unexploded land mines in the east of the country, so avoid visiting isolated places in this area.

It is illegal to sleep in your car, and you need a permit to pitch a tent anywhere outside of a campsite.

Dress

Dress in simple, clean, and modest clothes. Don't flaunt your designer labels or expensive accessories—not because of crime, but because you will be seen as pretentious.

Gifts and Tips

Always bring a wrapped gift when visiting a Croatian home (such as wine, coffee, cookies, or candy—most grocery stores have wrapping services). Give it to the head of the household. It will be opened in private and maybe not even mentioned again, but that does not mean that gifts aren't appreciated and very important.

Tipping is necessary in restaurants and should be between 10 and 15 percent.

The Czech Republic

considered overly familiar; it is interpreted as a direct attempt to insult or humiliate.

Czechs are very egalitarian so you will gain nothing by pulling rank or showing off your status, although academic titles are important. If a Czech compliments you, defer rather than saying thank you. Being down to earth and approachable is an important virtue.

Conversation

Czechs are very cultured, although they have quite a ribald sense of humor that isn't always politically correct.

Talk in a well-modulated voice and maintain good eye contact. Raising your voice will damage your credibility.

Don't be shy about attempting to speak a few words in Czech. They will be warmly received even if your pronunciation is far from perfect.

Czech history is complicated and painful, so avoid talking about politics and don't refer to the country as being either "developing" or in Eastern Europe. Prague is farther west than Vienna!

Meeting and Greeting

Always be punctual, even for dinner and social engagements.

Czechs are very warm and welcoming, although introductions can be quite formal. Use a firm handshake with good eye contact. This is viewed as honest and sincere. Shake hands with men and women, but wait for older people or women to initiate handshakes.

Don't use first names until you are invited to do so. Using a first name uninvited isn't just

Eating and Drinking

Lunch is the main meal of the day.

In a restaurant, the man always picks up the tab. If you are a woman, insisting on paying will embarrass and humiliate your male hosts.

Pubs have a distinct drinking etiquette that means you never run out of beer (the national drink—they consume the most beer per capita worldwide). Don't order from the bar; a waiter will come to your table and from then on he will slap a new beer in front of you every time your glass is nearly empty, until you tell him you've had enough. Expect an inch of head on your pint and always order draft beer. Never pour beer from one glass into another. Bottles are used when the draft runs out, and cans are an abomination. Drink only after you have toasted your companions.

Slurping noises during eating are considered very rude and uncouth.

Expect to share a table with strangers in a busy restaurant.

In restaurants you will be charged for the basket of bread or bowl of almonds on your table. This is normal—not a rip-off.

There is a wide range of cuisine, but you can expect to be served a lot of dumplings and potatoes during your visit.

Out and About

The culture is very masculine and includes showing courtesy to women, but you should not hold a door open. For a man, entering a room before a woman is a protective gesture.

Don't put your feet up. Keep them off of seats. On public transportation, always offer your seat to a woman or an older person. Cover your mouth when yawning or coughing. Avoid chewing gum in public.

Always ask permission before smoking.

Dress

Dress smartly without being ostentatious, although business dress is often quite relaxed.

Always remove your shoes upon entering a Czech home. You may be provided with slippers, but ensure that your socks are clean and don't take them off.

Gifts and Tips

Always bring a small gift, such as flowers or chocolates, when visiting a Czech home.

Add a 10 percent tip to a restaurant bill and tip 20 CZK for room service in a hotel.

Prices are cheap, but expect to be overcharged by Prague taxi drivers, who are notorious for their rudeness and inflated fares.

Always change money at banks or use an ATM machine. Be wary of money exchange offices, which charge high commissions and offer poor exchange rates. Never change money on the street; you will either be robbed or given worthless, obsolete notes.

Denmark

Meeting and Greeting

Shake hands with everyone in the room upon arrival and departure, including children. Greet women first.

Punctuality is paramount in business and social functions.

Conversation

Many Danish people speak English and German, but they prefer to speak English (unless you can speak Danish, of course).

Danes are quiet and shy before you get to know them. They dislike people who attract attention to themselves with loud or gregarious behavior. They are also very polite, and they say thank you a *lot*.

Like English humor, Danish humor is full of irony, so a comment such as, "This place is great" or "Fantastic weather" may mean the complete opposite.

Danes are Scandinavian, but they aren't Norwegian or Swedish, so don't offend by lumping them together or confusing them with these other nationalities.

Avoid criticizing high Danish taxes; they've heard it all before and they are proud of the social welfare system and social infrastructure that these taxes provide.

Eating and Drinking

The Danes have a word, *hygge* (pronounced *hooga*), that epitomizes the warm enjoyment of relaxed company. Nevertheless, formal dinner parties are quite common in Denmark and may involve place names, or if you are a man, a card telling you the name of your female dining companion. The guest of honor or the most senior man often makes a short speech after the meal to thank the host.

Food is often passed around on platters. Help yourself to a little of whatever appeals to you, but no more than you intend to eat. Use a knife and fork, even for the popular open sandwiches.

It is rude and wasteful to leave anything on your plate, but take your time eating. Dining is an important social occasion for the Danes and usually takes several hours.

When toasting, make eye contact with everyone in the group, say "Skål" ("Cheers"), sip your drink, and then make eye contact again.

Out and About

The Danes are very proud of their nationality. Their flag, the *Dannebrogen*, is the oldest national flag in the world, and you find it on sale everywhere. It makes appearances at dinner parties, in restaurants, and even at airports, where Danes wave flags at each other as they arrive.

Danes are not comfortable with a lot of physical contact. Avoid backslapping and other overt physical expressions, and maintain more than an arm's length of distance.

Don't use the OK sign, which is considered vulgar.

All tourists must register with the local police within 24 hours of arrival. (This will usually be sorted out by your hotel, but if you are staying with a family, you must take responsibility for this yourself.)

Dress

Dress smartly, with simple elegance, in well-made clothes, but avoid clothing that makes you stand out or broadcasts your wealth.

Complimenting other people's clothes is customary in many cultures, but not in Denmark, where such compliments are considered too intimate and inappropriate.

Gifts and Tips

Gifts are uncommon in business, but you should bring a gift when visiting someone's home. If you are giving flowers, leave them wrapped. Red roses are acceptable, but avoid white roses, which are associated with funerals. Alcohol is a good present because it is very expensive in Denmark.

Open any gifts you receive immediately and express your appreciation.

Restaurants usually include a service charge in the bill, but you may add another five percent for excellent service.

Egypt

Meeting and Greeting

An Egyptian greeting involves repeated expressions of welcome. A traditional greeting between two Arab men involves taking each other's right hands, placing the left hand on the other's shoulder and kissing each cheek.

However, more westernized men will use a simple handshake. Any kissing should only ever take place between members of the same sex.

Punctuality is not a priority; sometimes you're lucky if the person you're meeting shows up at all.

If a traditional Egyptian man does not introduce

his wife, take your lead from him. Always wait for the other party to initiate physical contact, such as a handshake.

Conversation
The personal space is very close. Don't back away if you feel your personal space is being invaded because this will be interpreted as coldness or rejection. There may also be a lot of touching during conversations.

The Arabic phrase for "No, thank you" is "Laa Shokran." You will need to use this expression frequently when you are approached by street vendors or children asking for money or inviting you to take their photograph (for money).

Egyptians have a healthy sense of humor, which can often be very self-critical. Don't make the mistake of joining in and criticizing others or their culture.

Don't bring up the subject of other people's families or wives, despite the fact that you may be asked some very personal questions by complete strangers (especially taxi drivers, who will quiz you on your faith, family life, and politics), which you may or may not choose to answer.

Eating and Drinking
Do not eat everything on your plate. Leaving a little food indicates the abundant hospitality of your host, who has provided more than you can eat. Don't add salt to your meal because this implies that the food isn't palatable.

Smoking in public is very common. Offer a cigarette to other members of your company. After a meal you may be offered a *sheesha*, or tobacco water pipe. You will see them everywhere, in cafes and on street corners. If you are not normally a smoker, be careful. Some sources claim that one *sheesha* is equivalent to smoking an entire pack of cigarettes.

Eat and pass plates of food with your right hand. (The left hand is reserved for unclean uses, such as going to the bathroom.)

Out and About
Do not look women in the eyes and do not talk to members of the opposite sex who are strangers; it will be interpreted as a come-on.

Politeness dictates that Egyptians will always refuse anything offered at least once before finally accepting. You should copy this custom because it is a way of discriminating between polite invitations and genuine ones. If someone invites you to his or her home, graciously decline; if the offer is genuine, it will be made again, after which you may accept. If you promise to visit someone's house, do not back out as this would humiliate your hosts.

When entering a house, stand to one side after you have knocked on the door or rung the door-bell, because it is impolite to look directly into the house when the door is first opened.

Always ask permission before taking some-one's photograph, especially a child; they will expect a tip. If you snap someone's picture without asking, don't be surprised if they follow you to ask for payment.

Egyptian males often walk hand in hand as a sign of friendship.

Do not point; it is very rude. Gesture with your whole hand.

Exposing the soles of your feet is very offensive. Keep both your feet on the ground when sitting.

"No" is not expressed by shaking the head, but with an upwards nod.

Dress

Dress to cover as much skin as possible. Men and women should keep shoulders covered at all times. Women should wear baggy clothes that do not emphasize their figure. Hemlines should be well below the knee, preferably ankle-length. A woman wearing inappropriate

clothing may receive lascivious stares or be groped by men.

Men should avoid visible jewelry, which is considered effeminate.

Always remove your shoes when entering a home or mosque. You will often be offered slippers, with a change of slippers for use solely in the bathroom.

Gifts and Tips

Give and receive gifts and tips with your right hand.

Tipping is a way of life in Egypt. If someone offers to carry your bags, or even so much as lifts them onto a bus, expect to be asked for a *bakshish* (tip). As a Westerner, wherever you go you will attract a lot of attention, especially from children. Don't give them money; it will either be taken by older children or it will compromise their education, because the parents will be encouraged to send them onto the streets rather than to school. Instead, give pens or pencils, which are greatly appreciated.

When invited to an Egyptian home, bring a small gift, such as baked goods or chocolates. Don't bring alcohol.

Finland

Meeting and Greeting

Punctuality is very important, especially in business. Arrive on time to social events.

Greet with a brief, firm handshake with direct eye contact and say your name. If you are introduced to a group of people, your host will usually make a public introduction so you won't have to shake everyone's hand. It is normal to shake hands with children.

Don't complicate the handshake by gripping the other person's elbow or touching his upper arm; it will make the person feel uncomfortable. Finns rarely embrace or kiss cheeks, and if so, only with close friends and family. When introduced to a married couple, greet the wife first. At a formal occasion the person

who received the invitation should greet the hosts first.

Do not use first names until specifically invited to do so. This is indicated when an older person shakes hands with a younger person and both parties say their first names and nod briefly while maintaining eye contact. From then on first names should always be used.

There is no special way to exchange business cards. Simply hand them over and put them in your pocket.

Conversation

Finns will often ask you what you think of their country, so do some homework and bone up on Finnish culture. Finns have a strong national identity and will feel slighted if you have no knowledge of Finnish achievements (despite the fact that they themselves may be quite insular regarding other cultures).

Small talk is not important and is not often used. Finns attach great importance to language and choosing words carefully, making silence preferable to empty chatter. It isn't necessary to keep the conversation flowing smoothly; Finns speak unhurriedly and with much pausing. If someone is talking, the biggest contribution you can make is to listen; don't interrupt. Always wait until the other person has finished talking. Don't be offended if a Finn sits for five minutes without saying a word. However, in general, the younger generation is far less reserved than their elders.

Talking to strangers in the street or on public transportation is unusual, although if you ask for directions you will usually find Finns to be very helpful.

Directness and honesty are important, so you should only extend invitations or make offers that you intend to follow through. Comments such as "We must do this again sometime" will be taken literally.

Eating and Drinking

Finns prefer to entertain at home rather than meet in restaurants. At a dinner party, the guest of honor sits to the right of the hostess and is expected to make a short speech of thanks on behalf of the other guests when the dessert wine or dessert has been served.

When a meal includes many courses, start with the cutlery on the outside and work your way in. Keep your knife and fork in your right and left hands, respectively, at all times; don't put your knife down to eat with your fork in the United States style. Don't start drinking the wine until the host has made a toast.

It is forbidden to smoke in public buildings and workplaces. Always ask permission in a private home; in a restaurant you should ask those around you whether they mind.

Out and About

Although Finns aren't big talkers, cell phone use in Finland is greater than in most other places in the world. (Nokia is a Finnish company not, as many believe, Japanese.) However, they are used with considerable discretion and respect for others. In public buildings you should always set your phone to vibrate. If your phone rings when you are at the theater, a restaurant, the library, or even a sports stadium, you may be asked to leave.

Finnish sauna is a way of life, and everyone has one at least once a week. The ratio of people to saunas in this country is about two to one. You will definitely be invited to share the experience during your visit—no clothes allowed, although men and women sauna separately (except couples). Be prepared to whisk each other with *vihta* (birch twigs).

Dress

Dress conservatively in good-quality, stylish clothes. Take your shoes off when entering a home.

Gifts and Tips

Tipping is not customary, due to the pragmatic belief that one should expect to receive good service anyway, without having to reward it by paying extra. However, a tip is always appreciated. You can either round up the bill or pay an extra 10 percent.

If you are invited to someone's house, a small gift such as flowers or wine will be appreciated.

France

Meeting and Greeting

Greet each person with a quick, light hand-shake (not a bone crusher or pumper), and use another handshake on departure. Friends and family will kiss each other on the cheeks (left and then right); you shouldn't initiate this, but be prepared to respond if someone greets you in this way (*la bise*). Wait for a woman to offer her hand first. When in doubt, shake hands.

The French often introduce themselves by stating their surname followed by their first name. They rarely smile on first meeting; this is not rude or standoffish, merely a more dignified and polite way of greeting. Business culture is especially formal in this respect.

Be prompt for appointments; punctuality is important.

Conversation

The French are polite and cultured and they love language, so if you take the time to learn a few phrases and pronounce them correctly, you will find French people very helpful. If you speak French incorrectly, you may be met with a shrug of apparent incomprehension. For instance, if you ask for "un baguette," it may seem obvious what you want, but a shopkeeper may appear to comprehend only once he has corrected your French—"Ah . . . une baguette."

Only use first name terms when invited. It is customary to address your elders with *Monsieur* or *Madame*. When entering a restaurant, shop, or hotel, greet by saying "Bonjour Madame/Monsieur" and "Au revoir" when you leave. Always say "Pardon" if you bump into someone on the street.

Being pushy will get you nowhere in France; you will simply be ignored. Say the magic words, "Excusez moi de vous derangez, Monsieur, mais j'ai un petit probleme. . . ." ("Pardon me for disturbing you, sir, but I have a small problem…"), and most people will be willing to help.

Don't keep smiling, making jokes, and being overly friendly too soon; you will gain more trust and respect if you are restrained and dignified at first. Friendship and trust are built slowly; over familiarity is considered superficial and is viewed with distrust.

In conversation (especially with bureaucrats and officials), cool logic will produce better results than hyperbole or emotional appeals. You will be judged on your intellect and your ability to discuss ideas. Business discussions are usually very protracted, and every option is carefully and seriously scrutinized. French

red tape is legendary. The French have a habit of politely restating their position so that a compromise can seem impossible.

"Merci" means "thank you," but when it is used in reply to a question, such as "Would you like some more?" it means "No, thank you." A response of "S'il vous plaît" means "Yes, if you please."

Eating and Drinking
Bread or breadsticks are an accompaniment to the main meal, so don't start nibbling until the food arrives.

Meals consist of many courses with smaller portions, so pace yourself and don't ask for seconds.

Attract a waiter's attention by tipping your head back slightly and saying "Monsieur." Never snap your fingers.

Do not eat food with your fingers (even sandwiches). Always use a knife and fork. Fruit should be peeled with a knife and eaten with a fork.

In a bar, take a seat and wait to be served a drink. If you buy a drink from the bar, it is cheaper, but you are expected to stay there to drink it.

Ice will only be added to your drink on request.

Don't help yourself to wine; your host or a wine waiter should ensure your glass is filled regularly. Expect the wine to change for each course.

Smoking is allowed in public places. Even in a restaurant you may see people smoking beneath the NO SMOKING sign.

Out and About

Good posture is very important and a sign of class. Keep your hands out of your pockets, don't slouch or chew gum, don't point with your whole hand, and don't use the OK sign (it means "zero" in France).

Don't browse through newspapers and magazines at a newsstand. If you want to read them, buy them.

Dress

Dress conservatively in good-quality, stylish clothes. Avoid wearing shorts unless you want to stand out as a tourist. Appearances matter; your social status is reflected by what you wear and how you wear it. Women never wear stockings in the summer.

Gifts and Tips

Since French business culture is quite formal, gifts should be carefully chosen to avoid embarrassing overfamiliarity. Don't include your business card.

When you are invited to a French home, don't bring wine—your host will have chosen a wine especially to complement the menu. An odd number of flowers (except chrysanthemums and carnations, which are unlucky, or red roses, which are romantic) or quality chocolates are acceptable gifts.

In restaurants a hefty VAT appears on your bill, so tipping is not obligatory. However, it is customary to leave a five percent tip (*pourboire*); 10 percent will ensure you receive even better treatment next time.

Germany

Meeting and Greeting

Punctuality is important, although arriving up to 10 minutes late is acceptable.

Exchange a firm, brief handshake with everyone in the group upon arrival and departure. Hugging and kissing on both cheeks is common only among good friends and family members.

Eye contact during the introduction is serious, direct, and should be maintained as long as the person is addressing you.

If a German stranger holds your eye contact, it does not mean that he will acknowledge you, because he does not expect anything from you. Because he doesn't know you, it is not logical to expect him to nod or smile, even politely.

Conversation

Small talk is not an important part of German interaction. They are more direct and say what they want, rather than wasting time with mere pleasantries.

Mingling is another rarity. Germans go to parties to mix with friends rather than to meet new people, so don't expect to be able to socialize with everyone in the room. Most likely the party will break up into close-knit groups, which can make a stranger feel excluded.

If a German asks, "How are you?" it is not a rhetorical question (as it is in the United

States, for example). Germans traditionally use "Wie geht es Ihnen" as a literal question that expects a literal answer.

Germans tend to receive compliments with slight suspicion, especially from anyone who is not a close friend.

Eating and Drinking

If you are formally invited out to dinner, then your host will expect to pay, and he or she won't even expect you to make a show of politely offering. You should definitely not fight for the bill! However, if you haven't been specifically invited, then you should expect to receive a separate bill and pay your own way.

Be patient when ordering a German beer. In some regions it can take 10 minutes to pour.

Don't expect your host to serve you. If you want more wine, for example, it is acceptable to pour it yourself—unless you are at a small dinner party, in which case the host might offer you more. Plates of food may be passed around the table, and each person should take what he or she wants, rather than sampling a little of everything for the sake of politeness.

Refusing food is okay. Germans are direct communicators and will expect you to be honest and direct.

In a busy restaurant, you may find yourself sharing a table with strangers, but you don't have to socialize with them during the meal, as might be the case in more relationship-oriented cultures.

When toasting, say "Zum Wohl!" with wine and "Prost!" with beer (both equivalents of "cheers"). Maintain eye contact until you have placed the glass back on the table. In a group, make eye contact with everyone individually.

Out and About

Always say hello when you enter shops, especially small ones.

Get used to recycling everything, even tea bags. Most plastic goes in the yellow trash (*Gelbe Tonne*); paper and cardboard go in the blue trash (*Blaue Tonne* or *Papiermüll*); glass is often separated into colors, e.g., green bottles (*Grünglas*) and white bottles (*Weissglas*). Biodegradable kitchen waste goes in the green trash (*Biotonne*), and anything else is gray (*Restmüll*).

Don't jaywalk. Only cross at crosswalks or traffic lights. German drivers won't always stop for you.

Despite the fact that Germany is a very regulated and law-abiding society, lining up and waiting their turn is not one of many Germans' strong points. It's first noticed, first served, like in a bar.

Germany is a time-dominated culture, so when it is your turn, keep your transaction efficient. For instance, at a supermarket checkout, if you don't get your groceries into your bags and move away quickly for the next person, you may get some disapproving looks.

Dress

Germans dress quite conservatively, in muted colors, both in business and socially. Even a simple trip to the grocery store or the mall requires a tidier appearance than sweatpants and T-shirt.

Gifts and Tips

Don't bother with gifts of beer, since the Germans are the beermeisters of the world; however, a good imported spirit or a quality wine is appreciated.

Don't give clothing, perfume, and other toiletries as gifts; these are considered too personal.

When tipping, round up to the next large number (e.g., €5.45 becomes €6 and €27.50 becomes €30).

Tip in a restaurant by adding to the bill, rather than leaving cash on the table. Beware of tipping too much, or you will look like a showoff.

Greece

Meeting and Greeting

Punctuality is fairly flexible. If you are a newcomer to Greece, try to arrive on time, but be prepared to wait for your Greek counterparts. Social events often begin up to an hour late and are open-ended.

Greet with a firm handshake and direct eye contact. When you know someone better you may embrace or kiss on both cheeks. You will typically be introduced to older people first (they are greatly respected in this culture), followed by men and then women. Shake

hands again with everyone in the group upon departure.

Titles are very important and respectful: Use *Keereeoss* (Mr.) and *Keereeah* (Mrs.) plus the family name (rather than first names).

Conversation

Greeks are very friendly and gregarious and will talk very openly about themselves and ask all sorts of personal questions. It is okay for you to reciprocate and ask your host similar questions.

Anger isn't always expressed directly; it might be vented with an ironic smile or a laugh.

Eating and Drinking

The drinking age in Greece is 16.

In many restaurants you are allowed (and even encouraged) to visit the kitchen to see how the food is being prepared and to decide what you would like to order. "Tea eeneh aftoe?" means "What is this?"

Groups of diners often order many communal dishes, which are placed on the table for everyone to help themselves. If you want more food, you may order it at any time during the meal, rather than only at the beginning. Greek waiters will leave you to enjoy your meal without continually returning to check that everything is okay. It is up to you to attract the waiter's attention if you need service.

Smoking during meals is not unheard of in Greece, although you should ask permission before lighting up.

In a Greek home, expect to be offered many seconds and thirds at meals. Eating well is a compliment to your hosts. If you are dining out, your host will usually pay the whole bill.

The most common toast is "Kalymata" ("Good health").

Greeks never rush their coffee; it is savored for at least half an hour. *Frappe* (chilled coffee) is very popular.

Out and About

When entering a shop or taverna, always acknowledge the owner with a "Kalimera" ("Good day") or "Kalispera" ("Good evening").

Raising an open palm at face level is insulting. The OK sign is considered a rude gesture with obscene connotations.

Greeks say no with an upward nod and yes by tilting the head from side to side. More con-fusing still, the Greek for yes is *Nai* and no is *Oci*.

If you compliment someone, you may see them puff breath through their lips. This gesture wards off the jealousy of the "evil eye." (Greeks are very superstitious.)

Greek men everywhere enjoy playing *Tavli* (backgammon), often very loudly and with good-natured taunting and banter.

In most toilets, paper goes in a special bin instead of being flushed away, to avoid blocking the pipes.

Dress

Business dress is conservative and formal, even during the summer; otherwise, dress is casual and comfortable, simple and elegant.

Gifts and Tips

Greek people are very generous. Don't make a big display of admiring an object or an ornament, or your host may feel obliged to give it to you.

When you are invited to a Greek home, make a big fuss over the children. Greece is a very child-oriented culture, so don't exclude them when talking to the adults.

Most restaurants add 15 percent service charge, and you may add a small tip for the waiter on the tray. In restaurants, the table clearers may be the proprietor's children, so leave some change on the table as well.

Hong Kong

Meeting and Greeting

In Hong Kong, a greeting will either be an English handshake or the Chinese bow or nod. Bowing deeper than another person is a mark of respect for that person's superior status. Men and women may shake hands. Greet the most senior person in a group first.

Punctuality is very important, especially in business. An exception is dinner engagements at someone's house, for which you should show up 30 minutes late. If you are with a group, arrive together.

Offer a business card with both hands, with the text facing away from you. When you receive a business card, it is polite to scrutinize it closely and then keep holding the card, rather than stuffing it into your pocket (which is rude and also signifies the end of the meeting).

A common Chinese greeting is "Have you eaten?" which is the equivalent of "How are you?" Always answer yes even if it's not true.

Conversation

If someone doesn't understand something, you may be met with a silent smile or even a yes, even though he or she doesn't have a clue what you are talking about.

Keep gestures to a minimum. The Chinese use very few gestures when speaking and may find such gestures distracting and irritating.

Saying no is hard for a Chinese person, who will prefer to say something like "perhaps" or "I'll think about it" in order to be polite. Expect to be let down very gently, since the Chinese are very diplomatic and will go out of their way to save face. If you need to discuss a sensitive subject, do so in private so you don't show someone up in public. Causing someone to lose face would be a disaster not only for your relationship, but for that person's whole family.

Eating and Drinking
Use the thick end of your chopsticks when taking food from a communal dish. Refusing food or drink is impolite, but don't dig around in a bowl looking for the best bits of food. Leave a small amount of food untouched to indicate that you are satisfied.

Eat rice by holding the bowl close to your face and scooping the rice into your mouth with your chopsticks. Leaving the bowl on the table is a sign that you are unhappy with the food. Never leave your chopsticks stuck in your rice; this is associated with death.

Hong Kong has some of the best restaurants in the world, but they are noisy! Also, the waiters can be very rude to everyone (not just visitors). Avoid lunchtime because you'll be obliged to jostle for a meal and eat your food at lightning speed.

It is polite to *offer* to pay, but your host will always settle up. Never suggest splitting the bill because this implies that your host cannot afford it. Instead, offer to return the hospitality in the future.

When the waiter serves you, tapping your index and middle fingers on the table twice means "Thank you." If you want more tea, turn the lid of the empty teapot upside down or hang it from the spout, and the waiter will give you a refill.

Ask for the bill by making circles with your index finger while pointing down at the table.

Burping and slurping are acceptable ways of expressing your enjoyment of the food.

Out and About
Generally, Hong Kong is a very safe country, but beware of pickpockets, especially in crowded areas—which means everywhere.

Jaywalking will result in a fine if you get caught. Cars have the right-of-way, so be alert.

Don't be upset if someone bumps into you and doesn't apologize. Hong Kong is busy and populous, and there is little respect for personal boundaries.

If you show a lot of interest in an item while shopping, you will be expected to buy it. So don't mislead the market sellers, but rather exercise discretion.

Step around the many puddles on the pavement unless you want to get dripped on by one of the numerous air conditioner outlets.

Chinese people don't smile much—not because they are miserable, but because they like to keep their emotions under control. Avoid public displays of affection.

Dress
Business suits in dark colors for men and subdued colors for women are appropriate.

Do not wear blue or white at social events; these colors are associated with death and mourning.

Gifts and Tips
Tipping is much more common in Hong Kong than in China, where it is often considered rude. However, it still is not obligatory. Giving gifts, on the other hand, is an integral part of Hong Kong protocol. If someone gives you a gift, you should reciprocate (always wrap a gift, but not in blue paper). You should open the gift in private.

If you are invited to a private home, bring whiskey, candy, or cookies.

Hungary

Meeting and Greeting

Exchange a firm handshake with everyone in the group upon arrival; this is optional upon departure. If someone has a professional title, it is polite to use it with their last name. Men kiss women on both cheeks.

You should always acknowledge, or even stand up, when an elder enters the room.

Hungarians are initially wary of foreigners. Friendship and trust are built slowly; over-familiarity is considered superficial and is viewed with distrust.

Conversation

Magyarul, the Hungarian language, is very difficult, so if you learn and use a few simple phrases it will be much appreciated.

"Hello/goodbye" (singular) is "Szia." "Hello/goodbye" (plural) is "Sziasztok." "Thank you" is "Köszönöm." "Good morning/day/night" is "Jó napot/estét/ejszakát." "Yes" is "Igen." "No" is "Nem."

Eating and Drinking

Dining in restaurants is mainly reserved for

special occasions. Keep your knife and fork in your right and left hands, respectively, at all times; don't put your knife down to eat with your fork in the United States style.

Don't start eating until someone (usually the host) has said "Jó étvágyat," an equivalent of "bon appetit." Thank the host at the end of the meal. Expect to be offered seconds, but it also is acceptable to ask for more food yourself.

Hungarians have a unique aversion to clinking glasses during a toast, in tribute to the 13 Hungarian generals who were arrested and jailed during the revolution of 1848. Their harsh Austrian captors used to clink glasses, so the Hungarians vowed to avoid this custom for the next 150 years. Even though the protest was officially fulfilled by 1998, it is often upheld.

Leave your napkin on the table, rather than place it in your lap. Keep your hands in view and your elbows off the table.

Alcoholic drinks are usually served after a meal, and it is impolite to refuse.

Don't eat in restaurants unless they list prices on their foreign language menus; otherwise, you may be considerably overcharged. In 1997, a Dutch tourist in Budapest was charged $6,000 (USD) for a meal!

Out and About
Bus tickets are bought from a ticket booth on the street and then validated with a machine on board; if you wait and pay the driver, the ticket is more expensive.

It is possible to hail a taxi, but it is more common to phone or go to a taxi stand.

Many trains are divided into compartments, and it is polite to ask those already occupying them if it is okay to sit down before you join them.

The legal limit for drinking and driving is very low, so abstain completely from consuming alcohol when you will be driving.

Dress
Dress smartly with simple elegance in well-made clothes, but avoid clothing that makes you stand out or broadcasts your wealth.

Gifts and Tips
When visiting a Hungarian home, bring flowers or candy for the host and small gifts for any children.

Tipping is widespread for everything from restaurants (15 to 20 percent) and taxi drivers (10 percent) to hairdressers, gas station attendants, and even doctors and dentists. If you don't leave a tip, it is a sign that you were dissatisfied with the service.

Iceland

Meeting and Greeting

The attitude toward punctuality is more casual in Iceland than in other parts of Europe. You will be forgiven for a little lateness, but you should still aim to be punctual for social engagements.

Use a firm handshake with good eye contact on arrival and departure. Icelanders are self-assured but quite reserved, and they may not initiate conversation. This doesn't mean they aren't friendly and welcoming; they will soon open up once you start talking.

If in doubt, say thank you, or "takk fyrir." It is a vitally important expression in Iceland.

Conversation

Icelanders are highly educated; the country has the highest literacy rate in the world. Conversation is direct and to the point, so small talk and pleasantries are not common. At all costs, avoid discussing the weather and definitely do not criticize it.

Directness and honesty is important, so you should only extend invitations or make offers which you intend to follow through.

When you hear two Icelanders speaking, you may be forgiven for thinking they are having an argument. It's something to do with the rhythm and consonants of the language.

Eating and Drinking

Restaurant food is unusual, diverse, and very high quality; Iceland is renowned for its fresh fish, Arctic lobster, organic lamb cuisine, and some fabulous cheeses. However the cost of dining out in Iceland (indeed, the whole standard of living) is the highest in Europe (although second helpings are often free).

Alcohol is very expensive, with a beer costing £6 (GBP)/$10 (USD). Spirits are even more costly. Don't offer to buy a round unless you want to part with some serious cash.

Don't leave the country without sampling *skyr*, which is a white, yogurt-like substance with a unique acquired taste.

Smoking is prohibited in public areas (public transportation and buildings), and all cafes and restaurants have nonsmoking areas. When visiting an Icelander's home, always ask permission before smoking.

Don't expect to buy coffee to go. Icelanders believe that coffee should be savored and appreciated, not chugged on the run.

If you are offered *Hákarl*, don't feel obliged to eat it. It is shark meat that has been buried and left to putrefy for up to six months.

Out and About

Icelanders work hard and play hard. Their working week is one of the longest in Europe, while Reykjavík, where more than 60 percent of the population lives, has some of Europe's hippest night life.

Dress

Businesspeople should dress smartly, and Icelanders tend to dress up to socialize. If you're going out on the town, only dress down in jeans and sweater if you want to stand out as a tourist, because everyone else will be wearing their best party gear.

Remove your shoes when entering someone's home.

Pack a range of warm-, cold- and wet-weather clothing. The weather is very changeable and temperature variations are pronounced, especially between daytime and nighttime. Don't forget to include your swimsuit and enjoy a dip in a geothermally heated swimming pool or one of the warm springs at any time of year.

Gifts and Tips

In Iceland, it is considered rude to give your hosts a gift when you are staying with them, although it is customary to bring flowers or a small gift if you are visiting for the first time.

Tipping in restaurants is not allowed. Service charges are included in the bill.

There is an old (but dying) custom of exchanging gifts on the first day of summer.

India

Meeting and Greeting

In India, the customary greeting is called a *namaste*, and it involves bowing slightly or nodding while holding your palms together below your chin. Handshakes are also used in business, but the *namaste* is the safest choice because you can use it in situations when you are unsure whether physical contact is appropriate.

Conversation

Indians are very friendly and gregarious and will start a conversation anywhere and ask all sorts of personal questions; it is okay for you to reciprocate and ask your host similar questions. Discussing your family is perfectly acceptable and will help to build trust.

Try to be accommodating and flexible at all times; if you express disagreement with

someone who doesn't know you well, you will be viewed as pushy or even hostile and aggressive. Avoid standing with your hands on your hips; this is an aggressive gesture. In conversation, an appeal to emotions and beliefs will produce better results than cool logic.

If you're stuck for conversation, talk about cricket, politics (except Pakistan), or movies. Do a little homework on all these subjects before visiting India; a bit of small talk will really break down cultural barriers. Avoid discussing poverty or religion unless you are showing a genuine interest in some aspect of religious observance. Do not insult anyone by confusing or comparing Indians with Pakistanis.

Indians are very polite so they have great difficulty saying no. Be sensitive to replies that might indicate a gentle negative, such as "We'll see." This apparent inability to commit to a negative decision is based on politeness, not deception.

Eating and Drinking

When someone offers you food or a drink, it is polite to refuse it at least once before accepting. After this, don't refuse an offer of food or drink because any rejection of hospitality is viewed as an insult. After eating, thanking your hosts is considered an abuse of hospitality because it implies that the food was not offered willingly. Instead, offer a genuine invitation to dine with you in the near future. Don't be surprised if your guests arrive late and bring uninvited guests. In the West this would be seen as taking liberties, but in India it is a sign that your friends like you enough to encourage others to enjoy your company and hospitality.

Always wash your hands before and after a meal. Hindus also rinse out their mouths before eating. Eat food with your right hand; the left hand is reserved for unclean uses such as going to the bathroom.

Don't offer anyone else, even a close friend or partner, food from your plate. The Western romantic image of offering a forkful of food to your lover would be viewed with disgust.

After a meal in a restaurant, you will be served a plate of seeds (usually anise or toasted fennel). Chew them to freshen your breath.

Out and About

Avoid public displays of affection with members of the opposite sex, including hugging someone to say hello. Many Hindus and Sikhs avoid all physical contact between the sexes, including handshakes. Muslim men must ritually cleanse before prayer if they touch a woman, so women should observe the practice of *namaste* when in doubt. You never see people kissing and hugging on the streets, although you may spot a little clandestine intimacy at some of the popular tourist sites.

Always arrive a few minutes late to a social function (unless it's an official function). Arrive about 15 minutes late to a dinner party.

When visiting someone's home, take special care to respect the customs and beliefs of others; your behavior will never be criticized while you are the honored guest.

The following are rude and should be avoided: winking, whistling, pointing or beckoning with your fingers, touching someone's ears or pointing your feet at someone. If your feet make contact with anybody else, you should apologize because feet are considered unclean.

Dress

Since the cow is sacred in India, wearing leather jackets, belts, or watch straps as well as carrying a leather purse may cause offense, especially in a place of worship.

Dress to cover as much skin as possible. Men and women should keep their shoulders covered. Women should wear baggy clothes that do not emphasize their contours. It is okay for Western women to wear a sari to a special event (such as a wedding); it shows you respect the culture and it will not be viewed as inappropriate as long as you have the confidence to wear it and you have chosen it carefully. (Ask an Indian female friend to help you shop.)

Gifts and Tips

In India, a tip or *baksheesh* is more about ensuring good service than rewarding it. For example, it might help to get you a seat on a train that is officially full. In a restaurant, a 10 percent tip after the meal is acceptable, but often a service charge is added to the bill.

If you receive a gift, open it in private. Wrap gifts with bright-colored paper; avoid black and white, which are unlucky. Don't give leather gifts.

Tipping a servant in a family home is acceptable, but check with the hosts because if you give the servant too much, it might undermine his or her relationship with the employer; what is loose change to you, may be several weeks' wages to the servant.

Israel

directness, warmth, and familiarity common in Israel. Israeli society is polychronic, which means that social interaction is governed by relationships, feelings, and intuition rather than objectivity or excessive formality. Your politeness, diplomacy, or rule-oriented (mono-chronic) behavior may well be interpreted as superficial and weak. Israelis are emotionally uninhibited and will express their feelings directly, without any of the formality or euphemisms to which you may be accustomed.

Your first experience of *doogri* will undoubtedly be at Customs, as you enter the country. You may be asked numerous questions, and you should expect to have your belongings and your person thoroughly searched in an uncompromising and assertive way. Be aware that this is for your own protection as well as that of the State.

Meeting and Greeting
Greet by saying "Shalom" (which means "Peace"), accompanied by a firm handshake. Be aware that personal space may be less than what you are used to, and do not step away if you feel that someone is standing too close. You may also find that there is more physical touching during conversation.

Punctuality is very relaxed. Expect to be kept waiting at the beginning of a meeting.

If an Orthodox Jew does not introduce his wife, take your lead from him. Always wait for the other party to initiate physical contact, such as a handshake.

Israelis have strong opinions and are not afraid to voice them, but do not be drawn into discussions about religion or politics. On the other hand, if you are in a heated discussion, don't be surprised if your Israeli counterpart suddenly breaks off the debate. It is his way of showing that a compromise is better than butting heads.

Eating and Drinking
Israelis observe strict dietary laws. Observance of the kosher diet involves, among other things, never mixing meat and dairy, and avoiding shellfish and meat from an animal without cloven feet. Kosher restaurants and cafes close on the Sabbath, so it can be very difficult to find

Conversation
Israelis take pride in their bluntness and directness, which they call *doogri*. This can often be interpreted as rudeness, aggressiveness, or arrogance. The positive side of this is the

anywhere to eat unless you plan ahead. Drinking alcohol is not a significant part of Israeli culture, and it is certainly not viewed as a key element of a good night out. You may raise eyebrows if two of you share a whole bottle of wine at a restaurant.

If you are not happy with the food in a restaurant, show a little *doogri* and express your dissatisfaction in a direct and honest way.

Out and About

You must carry identification at all times and show it if asked to do so by the authorities. Soldiers are everywhere. They are a fact of life in Israel (all Israeli men and women must do military service), and they are there for your protection.

You should always be acutely aware of and sensitive toward the religious sensibilities and customs. For example, the *Shabbat* (Sabbath) begins at sunset on Friday and is strictly observed until sunset on Saturday. Almost everything shuts down, including public transportation, shops, restaurants, and even El Al, the national airline. Avoid entering orthodox areas during this time.

Taking photographs of orthodox Jews or Muslims may offend, and you should never snap a picture of the military or police.

Drivers can't be relied on to stop at pedestrian crossings, and you may be shouted at for exercising your right to cross the road. Life is fast-paced. Get up to speed or you may be left behind and bewildered. If you bother lining up, you'll be waiting in a line for a long time. There is a first come, first serve mentality.

If you are a woman, avoid physical contact, especially with orthodox Jewish men. In stark contrast, some Israeli men will target lone women with whistles, insults, requests for sex, and will even grope them in public.

Dress

Business dress is less formal, with open-collar shirts and no jackets, but you should dress conservatively until you have established a norm.

Women should always dress modestly. Figure-hugging or flesh-revealing clothes should be avoided. In orthodox areas, inappropriate dress will be met with vocal disapproval—even spitting and stone throwing.

Both sexes should cover their shoulders and legs before entering a place of worship.

Gifts and Tips

Israelis are very generous, but in a business context gift-giving is kept to a minimum to avoid embarrassment.

When visiting an Israeli home, bring flowers or candy and small gifts for any children.

Tip 10 percent in restaurants.

Italy

Meeting and Greeting

Punctuality is fairly flexible. If you are a newcomer to Italy, try to arrive on time, but be prepared to wait for your Italian counterparts. Greet with a firm handshake and direct eye contact, and say "Buon giorno" ("good day") in the morning and "Buona sera" ("good evening") in the late afternoon and evening. Typically, you will be introduced to older people first (they are greatly respected in this culture). When you know someone better, you may embrace or kiss on both cheeks. Shake hands again with everyone in the group upon departure.

Only use first names when invited to do so. In business it is common for colleagues who have worked together for several years to still address each other using surnames.

Titles are very important and show respect: Use *Signore* (Mr.) and *Signora* (Mrs.) plus the family name (rather than first names).

Conversation

When answering the phone, say "Pronto," which means "ready," not "Buon giorno."

Italians use a repertoire of gesturing when they are speaking, and conversations are often very animated, noisy, and emotional. A passionate and eloquent speech will produce better results than cold reasoning as Italians

are guided by their emotions rather than by their intellect and rules. This means they can be quite flexible and inventive when problem solving, although business dealings are usually very protracted to allow friendship and trust to build.

Eating and Drinking

Breakfast is very small; lunch is usually the main meal of the day; and dinner is eaten very late. Cappuccino is a morning drink. After about 11 a.m. Italians switch to espresso.

Alcohol is rarely drunk on its own for pleasure. Wine should be sipped slowly, and usually only as an accompaniment to a meal or drunk with

friends in the evening. Italians pride themselves on being able to hold their liquor; getting drunk is an error, not an aim.

Sitting down to drink coffee is much more expensive than standing at the bar, which is why you will often see a crowd of Italians crowded at the bar drinking espresso.

When you buy a coffee or ice cream (*gelato*), you usually pay first, and then take the receipt and show it to the server.

It is polite to stay at the table until the meal is finished, rather than visiting the bathroom during the meal.

Don't mop up sauce or olive oil with your bread.

You may use it to gather a little sauce, but not to wipe the plate clean.

Eating well is a compliment to your hosts, so eat as much as you can and expect to be offered seconds and thirds.

Don't use a spoon to eat your pasta. Twirl it around your fork, using the side of the bowl if necessary.

Don't slurp up spaghetti.

Italians never cut lettuce. They fold it into a small parcel with their knife and fork.

Out and About
Italians have an expression, *bella figura*, which refers to the ability to conduct oneself with dignity, pride, and confidence in public. Be aware of the image that you are presenting to those around you. It will be noticed.

Lining up is optional, with much pushing and line-jumping.

There are feral cats all over Italy, especially in Rome. Don't approach them; they are wild animals and may carry disease.

If you place your hand on your stomach and make a face, it means you dislike someone or something. Rubbing your chin with your fingers and then flicking them forward is an expression of anger or frustration.

Chewing gum is considered vulgar. Smoking, on the other hand, is widespread, even in nonsmoking sections in restaurants.

Dress
When in Italy wear the best shoes you can afford and keep them well polished. Dress in good-quality, stylish clothes (not shorts). Appearances matter; your social status is reflected by what you wear and how you wear it.

Both men and women wear a lot of accessories, such as jewelry, expensive watches, and ties. Women tend to wear darker colors and accessorize with flashes of color. They don't wear stockings in the summer. Both sexes wear cologne or perfume.

Gifts and Tips
In business, only give a gift if you have already received one; otherwise, it might be interpreted as a bribe. Open any gifts immediately.

When you are invited to someone's home, an odd number of flowers (except chrysanthemums, carnations, or red roses) or quality chocolates are acceptable gifts.

In most restaurants a 10 to 15 percent service charge (*servizio*) is added to the bill, and tipping is not obligatory, although you may choose to leave an extra five percent for excellent service.

Tip the people sitting outside public restrooms 25 to 50 euro cents.

Japan

Meeting and Greeting

Japanese culture is dominated by etiquette, but don't worry about causing an international incident if you make a mistake. You won't go far wrong as long as you get into the habit of considering others (and the group) before yourself.

Punctuality is essential. Show up on time and you will rarely, if ever, be kept waiting.

Japanese people often shake hands, knowing that it is what you are used to, but it is polite to adopt their custom of bowing, which expresses both respect and humility. When bowing to someone of higher status, you should bow slightly lower than that person. In shops, a nod is sufficient. A bow is also used for apologies (which are frequent) and to say goodbye.

Do not use first names until invited, and don't embarrass others by asking them to call you by your first name until you have met a few times.

Present your business card with both hands. When someone gives you theirs, spend a moment reading it carefully before placing it in a card case or on the table. Don't just stuff it into your pocket unread, and don't write on it.

Age equates to high status, so show respect for the elderly.

Conversation

Talk quietly at all times, and keep your facial expressions to a minimum. Never show your anger or even irritation.

Japanese people are so polite that they apologize frequently, even when an apology seems unnecessary. You should do the same; say "Sumimasen," which means "I'm sorry." The Japanese also have great difficulty saying no, so be sensitive to replies that might indicate a gentle negative, such as "I'll consider it." Don't put others on the spot by asking questions that are difficult to answer. Remember, you can never be too polite in Japan.

A long pause in the conversation is not a sign of discomfort, but a moment that allows for thought. Also, if someone crosses his arms or closes his eyes while you are talking, it is a sign that he is considering your words carefully.

Eating and Drinking

After being seated in a restaurant, you'll be presented with a wet towel called an *oshibori* (hot in the winter or refreshingly cool in the summer) for wiping your hands.

In a restaurant, your host will usually pay. The person with the highest status sits at the center of the table, and the guest of honor sits to the right of the host. If you find yourself sitting next to the door, then you are the least important person in the group.

Use the thick end of your chopsticks to help yourself from the many communal dishes on the table. It is polite to try a little of everything, or else make an excuse (e.g., a food allergy). At the end of the meal, leave a little food to show that you are satisfied. Never pass food to someone else with your chopsticks or stand your chopsticks up in your rice; both gestures are associated with funerals.

Don't gesticulate with your chopsticks or point them at anyone. When you aren't using them, place them on the chopstick rest.

Slurping is an acceptable way of tasting and cooling noodles, soup, or tea.

Don't pour your own drink. Wait for others to give you a refill, and return the gesture. If you've had enough to drink, leave the cup half full or turn it upside down. To make a toast, say "Kanpai" before drinking. Tea is served at the end of the meal.

Don't eat food on the move. If you buy take-out food, stand or sit down to eat.

Out and About
Japanese women cover their mouths when laughing. When talking about yourself, point to your nose, not your chest.

Lining up is extremely successful here. Wait your turn and don't push.

Remove your shoes and wear the slippers provided when entering a Japanese home. Change in and out of bathroom slippers when going to the bathroom.

Check out one of the high-tech toilets if you get the chance; with all those buttons and neat gizmos, it's the next best thing to training to be an astronaut.

Smiling is often used to disguise negative emotions, such as embarrassment or disapproval; it is not always a sign of amusement. Head scratching is often used in the same way.

It is impolite to blow your nose in public, and using a handkerchief rather than a disposable tissue is considered unsanitary.

Dress
Business dress is conservative, but pastel shirts are becoming more acceptable. Women should wear minimal perfume, makeup, and jewelry.

Gifts and Tips
Gift-giving is integral to Japanese culture, especially in business. Present and receive gifts with both hands. If you are giving to an individual, do so in private so you don't make anyone else feel left out or snubbed. It is customary to play down the importance of the gift as you present it by saying it is "tsumaranai mon" (boring, nothing special). Gifts are usually given at the end of a visit. You will often be showered with gifts upon your departure after staying at someone's home.

Tipping is rare in Japan, and a service charge is added to restaurant bills.

Mexico

Meeting and Greeting

Mexicans place much importance on personal and family relationships, so trust and respect, especially in business, are built up by your ability to interact with others, not by your credentials.

A Mexican handshake is a brisk, firm snap. Say "Buenos días/tardes/noches" for "Good morning/afternoon/evening or night" or "Hola, cómo estás" ("Hi, how are you?").

Friends greet each other with a touch on the elbow or a full-on *abrazo*, which is a bear hug with much backslapping. Don't be surprised if someone gives you a hearty *abrazo* after only the second meeting. Mexicans are very friendly.

Winking and whistling (called the *piripo*) is quite common between men and women on meeting. Cheek-kissing is also popular.

Always use *Señor* (Mr.) and *Señora* (Mrs.) or *Señorita* (Miss) plus the paternal family name until you are invited to switch to first names.

Punctuality is very flexible in Mexico. It is common to arrive half an hour late for social events. The main adjustment you will have to make will be adapting to the slow pace of life.

Conversation

Spanish is the main language, but about a third of the population also (and sometimes exclusively) speaks the indigenous Indian languages of the Aztecs and Maya. Any attempt to speak Spanish, however inadequate, will be appreciated.

Familiarize yourself with the concept of *mañana*, which means "tomorrow" and is a habitual response to questions that require a definite answer. If you want to know when your car will be fixed, it will always be *mañana*. This can seem like stalling or laziness, but actually Mexicans are reluctant to disappoint. If you ask someone for directions, they would rather send you in the wrong direction than offer no help at all. Maybe can often mean no.

If you hear someone saying "psst-psst," they are trying to get your attention; this is not considered rude.

Eating and Drinking

When paying in shops and restaurants, always place cash or credit cards into the hand of the person who is serving you. It is rude to place it on the counter.

Out and About

Personal space is small. Mexicans stand close, so don't back away; they will think you are being shy and quickly close the gap again. Or, worse, they will think you are being unfriendly.

If you are invited to someone's home, don't discuss business unless the subject is raised.

It is respectful to keep eye contact short and infrequent, especially with your elders. Holding a stare is confrontational, as is standing with your hands on your hips.

Dress

Business dress is conservative, with dark suits for men and smart, feminine skirts and blouses along with nylons and high heels for women.

Gifts and Tips

Gift-giving is not an integral part of Mexican business culture, but a small gift is not inappropriate. However, if a businessman offers a gift to a woman, he should say it is from his sister or his wife to avoid potential embarrassment.

Bringing a small gift when you are invited to someone's house is optional. Avoid red or yellow flowers (according to Mexican folklore, the former cast spells, the latter signify death); also avoid silverware from another country, as Mexican silver is world-famous.

Morocco

Meeting and Greeting

Greet by shaking hands and saying "Salam," or "peace be unto you." Moroccans often follow this by tapping their hearts with their hands. Members of the same sex often kiss their friends once on one cheek and twice on the other.

Conversation

In Morocco, the expression "any friend of yours is a friend of mine" is a good description of the social life. Once you have some friends here, you will quickly make more.

Eating and Drinking

Even though it is a Muslim country, you can buy beer and wine in many restaurants, some cafes, and specialty stores that open for a few hours each day.

Mint tea is very popular. It is usually drunk very hot with plenty of sugar.

Avoid traveling to Morocco during Ramadan because daytime fasting will make it harder to find food and drink. During Ramadan you shouldn't eat, drink, or smoke in the presence of locals until sunset. However, the nighttime feasting helps to make up for the depravation experienced during daylight.

Moroccan women do not smoke in public.

Always drink bottled water. The locals drink the water, but their stomachs are accustomed to the microbes. Keep your mouth closed while showering, and use bottled water for brushing your teeth.

When invited to a family meal, use the pitcher to symbolically wash your hands. Eat food with your right hand; the left hand is reserved for unclean uses such as going to the bathroom. Clearing your plate means that you want more to eat. You will always be offered seconds, so leave some room for more because refusing food and drink is considered rude.

Out and About

Some parts of Morocco (e.g., Casablanca) are more Western than most other Muslim countries, but you should show respect for their religious customs.

Always barter with street vendors. Ask them to make the first offer, start your haggling at 10 percent of the asking price, and never pay more than half of the original price. In the West is it customary to handle and inspect goods to decide whether you want them. In Morocco, your actions will be interpreted as an intention to buy. If you show a lot of interest in an item and then walk away, the vendor will think it is part of your bartering act and will pester you, so be wary of giving the wrong message.

When taking a taxi, long trips are paid for at the beginning, while short trips are paid for at the end.

Members of the same sex hold hands in public as a sign of friendship, but public displays of affection between the sexes are inappropriate and may draw the attention of the authorities.

Always ask permission before taking someone's photograph. If they agree, they will often expect payment. The Berber people are very wary of cameras, believing that they capture a person's soul, whereas the performers in places such as Marrakech (snake charmers, dancers, etc.) rely on your tips to make a living.

If you see a bottle floating in a squatting toilet, leave it alone. It is there for a good reason—to deter passing rats from taking an interest in your behind.

Unless you are a Muslim, you will not be allowed inside any of the mosques except the Great Mosque in Casablanca. You can visit other monuments for free on Fridays, unless you want to avoid the crowds.

Dress

Morocco is a modern and progressive Muslim country, so dress codes vary depending on age and location. On the beach or in touristy places such as Marrakech, Casablanca, or Rabat, you'll see young locals wearing bikinis and miniskirts, while in more remote areas, anything less modest than the traditional *jeelaba* will draw stares and unwelcome attention. Use your discretion and if in doubt, dress to cover as much skin as possible, especially your collarbone. Keep shoulders covered at all

times. Women should wear baggy clothes that do not emphasize their contours. A woman wearing inappropriate clothing may receive lascivious stares or be groped by men.

If you are a single woman wishing to avoid unwelcome male attention, wear a fake wedding ring.

Gifts and Tips

If children pester you to take their photograph, they want money. Instead, give pens or pencils, which are greatly appreciated.

Tipping is unavoidable. You will be deluged by offers of help everywhere in exchange for small tips. It is a good idea to keep your loose change and bills separate so you don't pull out a flashy roll of cash when you only intend to part with a few coins.

The Netherlands

Meeting and Greeting

The Dutch are very warm and welcoming, although introductions can be quite formal, and often don't include a lot of smiling, Use a firm handshake with good eye contact. Shake hands with men and women. Close friends (except two men) may kiss each other on the cheeks three times (left, right, left).

Punctuality is very important, especially in business. Arrive on time to social events.

The Dutch are sticklers for good time management and will not appreciate a sudden change of plans.

Conversation

Discussion of politics is welcome in the Netherlands. But beware, because the Dutch are very well informed. However, it is very rude to ask how someone votes in an election.

Despite being very individualistic, the Dutch are attracted to logic and facts, so expect a hyperbolic emotional speech to be viewed with confusion and embarrassment. Speak in a calm and composed manner at all times, and be direct and straightforward. Raising your voice, gesturing, or becoming too animated is unwelcome.

Complimenting other people's clothes or achievements is customary in many cultures, but not in the Netherlands, where compliments are thought to highlight an individual above

85

the group. Consensus and equality are very important.

Eating and Drinking
Dinner is eaten early. An invitation for 6:30 p.m. usually means dinner, whereas an invitation for 8 p.m. is often for after-dinner drinks. If you're not sure, check with your host.

The host and hostess sit at opposite ends of the table, and the guests of honor sit to the right of the hosts. Eat with your knife and fork, even for fruit, pizza, and sandwiches.

There is a difference between a cafe and a coffee shop. Both sell coffee and food, but in the latter you can also legally buy and smoke marijuana or hash oil. Don't take or use the drugs outside of this establishment.

Out and About
When entering a small shop, you should acknowledge everyone and say hello. In other respects the Dutch are quite reserved and will not spontaneously enter into conversations in public with strangers.

Don't keep smiling, making jokes, and being overly friendly too soon; you will gain more trust and respect if you are restrained and dignified at first. Friendship and trust are built slowly; overfamiliarity is considered super-ficial and is viewed with distrust. Compromise and consensus are very important, but so are

asserting one's own rights and making indi-vidual choices while tolerating the lifestyles and cultures of others.

Directness and honesty are important, so you should only extend invitations or make offers on which you intend to follow through.

Dress
Dutch people are smart dressers who believe in presenting a clean and elegant image. Good taste and modesty are valued above showiness and ostentatious displays of wealth. Rich people do not flaunt their wealth by wearing conspicuously expensive clothes and accessories.

Business dress varies from the conservative to very casual, depending on the profession. In some cases, the more senior employees dress more casually than those in lower positions.

Gifts and Tips
If you are invited to dinner at a Dutch home, arrive on time and bring some flowers or a modest gift for the hostess. If you bring wine it will probably be left unopened because your host will already have chosen wine especially to compliment the menu.

In restaurants a service charge of 10 percent is automatically added to the bill. You may add up to 10 percent for excellent service, but it is not obligatory.

New Zealand

Meeting and Greeting

Greet with a firm handshake while maintaining good eye contact. New Zealanders may often say "G'day," but don't wear out the greeting yourself because it can sit uncomfortably and appear a little patronizing from a foreigner.

When greeting Maori people, a handshake is customary, although the traditional greeting is called a *hongi*—women are kissed on the cheek, and men press noses together with eyes closed while making a "mm-mm" sound. "Tena koe" is Maori for "Hello" when you are addressing one person. Use "Tena koutou kotoa" for more than one person.

Do not maintain prolonged eye contact with Maori people; Polynesians interpret this as confrontational.

Conversation

New Zealanders are friendly, open, and relaxed. Just like Australians, they dislike anyone who thinks he or she is better than others. This is called the *tall poppy syndrome* (also known as the great Kiwi clobbering machine), referring to the way poppies that grow taller than their surroundings tend to get picked first. New Zealander society is very egalitarian, so anyone attempting to pull rank or show off his or her achievements will be quickly cut down to size.

Also, don't confuse Kiwis (New Zealanders) with Australians. They are as different as Canadians and Americans.

Eating and Drinking

There are very tight restrictions on bringing

animal products, food, and plants into the country. Even candy may be confiscated. If you are carrying a large quantity of medication, get a doctor's note to prove that you require the medication.

When dining out, expect to pay for your share unless you have been specifically invited out for a special treat at your host's expense.

Don't stand on ceremony at a barbecue. Your hosts will expect you to get "stuck in" and enjoy yourself without asking for permission at every step. Serve yourself and make yourself at home. If the invitation says you should bring a plate, it isn't a warning about a shortage of dishes; it means you should bring a plate of food. That way, when everyone shares, there will be enough to go around.

Out and About
Don't arrive unannounced at someone's house. Arrange a visit beforehand.

Respect Maori culture. If you are asked to stay away from certain sacred sites, please obey this request.

Personal space is large. Maintain at least an arm's length of distance.

Kiwi men aren't big on hugging, touching, or other friendly expressions of physical contact. If you consider yourself a sensitive man, then spare the feelings and embarrassment of others and take your lead from your hosts.

Kiwis drive on the left side of the road. Tourists here are especially prone to having accidents. Drivers become careless when traveling long distances, and there are other hazards such as flocks of sheep. Most bridges are only wide enough for one vehicle, so read the signs to see who has the right of way before crossing. (If the red arrow points in your direction, you must yield to oncoming traffic.)

If you rent a car on North Island, you can't take it to South Island, and vice versa. The ferry is expensive, but it's cheaper if you reserve in advance.

Dress
When visiting the volcanic plateau on the North Island, be prepared for your clothes to smell like rotten eggs (sulfur) for several days afterward.

Business dress is quite conservative, although it may vary depending on the profession. Take your lead from those around you.

The winter months are from May to September. New Zealand is farther south than Australia, and the weather is more changeable, especially in alpine areas, so dress in layers and bring waterproof gear.

Gifts and Tips
Tipping is not a New Zealand custom, but it is still appreciated. In a restaurant you may add 10 percent to the bill for excellent service.

Norway

Meeting and Greeting

Punctuality is very important in business and for social events. You must call ahead if you are going to be late.

Greet everyone in the room with a firm handshake and good eye contact and say, "God dag," or "good day." Shake hands again when you leave, rather than using a group wave.

Even good friends rarely hug and kiss, so avoid bear hugs and backslaps even with those you know well, unless they initiate them. Allow plenty of personal space between yourself and others unless the beer has been flowing, in which case Norwegians get very touchy-feely.

Keep hand gestures to a minimum. Norwegians can be quiet and shy until you know them well, so don't draw attention to yourself with gregarious behavior. Norwegians, like many Scandinavians, like to party hard on weekends.

Most people will use *du* (you) if they don't know you well. *Herr* (Mr.) or *Frue* (Mrs.) is rarely used.

Norwegians are Scandinavian, but they aren't Danish or Swedish, so don't offend people by lumping them together or confusing Norwegians with these other nationalities.

Conversation

Norwegians are polite and straightforward; they appreciate directness in conversation. Although they can appear reserved at first, they will quickly become warm and friendly as you gain their trust.

At a dinner party, don't wait for the host to introduce you to others; it is up to you to break the ice.

Don't call the Sami people Lapps or Laplanders. (It is akin to calling an Innuit person an Eskimo.)

Eating and Drinking
Eating and drinking out are very expensive in Scandinavia, and especially Norway, so Norwegians like to save money by gathering at someone's house for a *vorspiel*, or pre-party, at about 8 p.m. to have a few drinks before hitting the town around midnight. Going to someone's house for a drink after closing time is called a *nachspiel*, or after-party.

When dining at home, don't start eating before the host. To toast, lift your glass, catch someone's eye, take a sip, look back at that person, and nod before putting the glass down.

Before leaving the table after a meal, always thank the hostess or cook by saying "Takk for maten," or "thanks for the food." The guest of honor, seated to the left of the host, will often make a short speech of thanks (called a *Skål*). The next time you meet your host you can even say "Takk for sist." ("Thanks for the other night.")

Out and About
The standard of living is very high. Norwegians often take a trip to neighboring Sweden to take advantage of the lower prices.

When driving, don't expect Norwegians to use turn signals.

When visiting an office, don't be surprised to see that someone's dog is sleeping under his or her desk.

Norwegians are not keen at all on working overtime; most people clear out of their offices before the day finishes at 4 p.m. (The working day starts at 8 a.m.)

Dress
Norwegian men dress very casually, even at work, and may even wear jeans to a meeting. For fancier social occasions it is customary to arrive in a pair of outdoor shoes and change into dressier indoor shoes upon arrival (especially when it's been snowing). For casual visits remove your shoes at the door.

Many restaurants expect you to hang up your coat or hand it in to the coat-check room before being shown to your table.

Gifts and Tips
Bring a small gift when you are invited to someone's house. Flowers, chocolate, or wine are acceptable.

A service charge is included in the bill, but a 10 percent tip is acceptable for excellent service. Or, you can round the bill up to the nearest 10 or 25 NOK.

Pakistan

Meeting and Greeting

You will usually be greeted with a handshake and the words "Assalaam-u-Alaikum" ("May peace be upon you"), to which you should reply "Waalaikum assalaam" ("And peace also upon you"). Close friends of the same sex may embrace. Women greet each other with a handshake or hug. Men should not shake hands with women.

Be punctual to meetings with Pakistanis, but don't expect them to be on time.

Conversation

Asking about family is acceptable and polite, but do not show too much interest in the women. If you learn and use a few words of Urdu, it will be much appreciated.

Don't make a big deal about the poverty. Pakistanis know their country is poor; it is very rude to keep reminding them of it.

Eating and Drinking

Pakistanis are very friendly and generous and will often invite you home for a meal, where you will be treated as an honored guest. A refusal is impolite, although you should not overstay your welcome—leave soon after you have finished eating.

When someone offers you anything, it is polite

to refuse it before accepting. A Pakistani may offer you something that he does not have or cannot afford to give, so be sensitive to all offers by declining several times. If the offer is genuine it will be repeated. (In the case of food, the item may be thrust into your hands.) Don't accept drinks from people on buses or trains; there have been several cases of drugging and mugging.

Eat food with your right hand; the left hand is reserved for unclean uses such as going to the bathroom.

Pakistan is largely Muslim, while India is largely Hindu, so the Pakistani diet is dominated by meat (especially beef) and alcohol and pork are forbidden, while Indian food is often vegetarian. Do not insult someone by confusing or comparing Indians to Pakistanis.

Out and About
Non-Muslims are allowed to visit mosques, but should dress appropriately (covering arms, legs, and hair and removing shoes) and avoid the five daily prayer times. You can even use a camera as long as you don't use a flash—also, don't take pictures of the women.

Lone female travelers will be frowned upon and shunned because only loose women travel unaccompanied.

Avoid public displays of affection with members of the opposite sex, including hugging someone to say hello. Muslim men must ritually cleanse before prayer if they touch a woman.

The following are rude and should be avoided: winking, whistling, pointing or beckoning with your fingers, or showing the soles of your feet. If your feet make contact with anybody else, you should apologize; feet are considered unclean.

Women always take precedence in lines and seating.

Dress
Dress to cover as much skin as possible. Women should keep their shoulders covered and wear a scarf. They also should wear baggy clothes that do not emphasize their contours. Hemlines should be ankle-length.

The common garment for both sexes is the *shalwar qameez*, a cotton tunic worn over loose clothing. The garment is usually made of cotton, and the women wear bright colors and a *dupatta* (scarf), while the men wear more muted shades and, if traditional, a turban, which varies from region to region.

Gifts and Tips
Tipping for good service is not customary except in the larger hotels and restaurants, which add a service charge of 10 percent to the bill. However, as in India, a *baksheesh* helps to get things done.

Poland

Meeting and Greeting
Greet with a firm handshake and maintain good eye contact upon arrival and departure, and say "Czesc" ("Hello") or "Do widzenia" ("Goodbye"). Women and close friends greet each other with kisses. Older Polish men might kiss a woman's hand.

First names are reserved for family and close friends. Otherwise, you should use the last name, preceded by *Pan* (for men) or *Pani* (for women, regardless of marital status). If you are invited to use first names, it is still common to use these prefixes.

Conversation
Personal and family relationships are every-thing, so outsiders will be expected to prove themselves to build trust and respect by conforming to the formal culture and conducting themselves with dignity and moral fiber.

Eating and Drinking

Tea is very popular in Poland. Some older Poles sip their tea through a sugar cube held between their front teeth.

Polish vodka is world-famous, and Poles have a tendency to believe that no one can handle their vodka like they can. Beware of drinking too much—Polish hospitality will last much longer than your ability to stay upright. The most common toast is "Na zdrowie" ("Health"), but you may also hear "Stolat" ("100 years—long life").

Before a meal, especially when dining at someone's home, you should say "Smacznego," or "bon appetit," before beginning to eat. After the meal, thank your host for the food and the other guests for dining with you by saying "Dziekuje" ("thank you") or "Dziekuje bardzo" ("thank you very much").

Keep your knife and fork in your right and left hands, respectively, at all times; don't put down your knife to eat with your fork in the United States style.

Poles don't talk much while eating, but it is customary to stay at the table and chat after the meal is finished.

Out and About

Hand gestures are minimal, but it isn't necessary to restrict your own gesturing if that's what you're used to.

Women often walk hand in hand or with linked arms in public as a sign of friendship. It is quite common to see young couples making out on park benches, since most of them still live with their parents and other members of their extended families, so privacy at home is hard to find.

Lining up doesn't happen in Poland! It's a free-for-all.

Bathrooms are often marked with an upside-down triangle for men and a circle for women.

Dress

People take pride in their appearance, so dress well and present a clean and proper image.

In general, you should remove your shoes before entering a Polish home.

Gifts and Tips

If you are invited to dinner at a Polish home, arrive on time and bring an odd number of flowers or a modest gift for the hostess.

Service is not included in a restaurant bill. Tip 10 percent or round up the amount. However, when the waiter collects your money, if you thank him by saying "Dziekuje," it actually means "Keep the change." It can be very awkward to get your money back if you say this unintentionally.

Portugal

Meeting and Greeting

Always shake hands (though not too firmly) with everyone in a group, even if you are well acquainted. Women often kiss each other on both cheeks, and men may kiss women in this way. However, there is no fixed rule, so it is safest to stick with a handshake initially. Shake hands again upon departure.

Don't use first names until you're invited to do so; until then use *Senhor* and *Senhora* with the last name. People in Portugal are known as Dr. if they have a bachelor's degree.

Conversation

Eye contact is much more sustained than in other cultures. At first this may make you feel uncomfortable, or you may think that others are staring, but it is important to persevere with this high level of visual contact, or else you may be viewed as unfriendly or untrustworthy.

When hanging up the telephone, the Portuguese perform a peculiar ritual that seems to involve saying goodbye and excuse me ("Com license") as many times as possible; it goes something like "Goodbye, excuse me, goodbye, excuse me, bye, bye…" However, if you dial a wrong number, the person at the other end will put the phone down without uttering a word.

The Portuguese seem to be very impressed by and interested in foreigners, so you should have little difficulty establishing a rapport.

It is okay to talk about your family, even to those you don't know well; it is also acceptable to use humor to get to know people (unlike in some countries, where polite formality is more appropriate at first). Don't talk about religion or finances/salaries.

Eating and Drinking
In a restaurant the waiter will bring bread and a small bowl of appetizers, such as olives; these are not complimentary and if you eat them, they will appear on the bill.

Keep your knife and fork in your right and left hands, respectively, at all times; don't put down your knife to eat with your fork in the United States style, and do not eat with your fingers. When you have finished eating, cross your knife and fork on your plate.

The waiter will only bring the bill when you ask for it; it is very rude for a waiter to present the bill before it has been requested. Often you will find that a member of your party has sneaked off to pay the bill already. The bill will only be itemized if you ask for it to be a *factura*; otherwise, you will receive a cash-register receipt.

Out and About
If someone flicks his or her fingers underneath the chin, it means "I don't know" or "I don't understand." The same gesture using just the thumb means that something no longer exists or has died.

If people kiss the side of their index finger and then pinch their ear, it means they enjoyed their meal and wish to pay their compliments to the chef (or host).

Portuguese and Spanish bullfighting differ; in Portugal, the bull is wrestled to the ground by a bunch of men and is killed in private after the audience has left.

Yawning or stretching in public is rude.

Always write in blue or black ink; for some reason, the red pen is only associated with schoolteachers' markings, and using it is rude in any other context.

Dress
Smart casual wear is adequate for most situations outside of business, although you should dress up more to go to the theater or a restaurant. Portuguese men only ever wear long-sleeved shirts with a tie.

Gifts and Tips
In a restaurant, the service charge is not included in the bill, so a 10 percent tip is customary.

Gift-giving in business is common; if you are given a gift, it is for your personal use and is not to be shared with the rest of your colleagues. Open gifts immediately in front of the giver.

Romania

Meeting and Greeting

The most usual greeting is a handshake, but a Romanian man may kiss a woman's hand, and it is not uncommon for close male friends and family to hug.

Outside of the major cities, strangers in the street will say "Buna ziua" ("good day"), and you should return the greeting. Communities are close knit, so a villager will assume that you must be staying with someone he or she knows, and therefore you deserve a welcome.

Romanians often use *Domnul* (Sir) and *Doamna* (Madam) before the last name, although the younger generation tends to be on first-name terms. With older people you should use this polite address unless you are invited to switch to first names.

Conversation

Few subjects are off limits, so don't be surprised if you are asked about your age, politics, income, or religious beliefs.

Eating and Drinking

Keep your knife and fork in your right and left hands, respectively, at all times; don't put down your knife to eat with your fork in the United States style. Keep your hands on the table, but not your elbows.

During the summer, Romanians often mix their wine with sparkling mineral water (*sprit*), and the waiter may ask if you would like your wine served this way. Drinks are served without ice unless it is specifically requested.

To make a toast, say "Noroc" ("Cheers"). Before eating it is polite to wish your companions "Pofta buna" ("Good appetite").

If you decline food, your host may assume you are being polite and serve you anyway, so it is important to distinguish between a polite refusal and a genuine one.

Drinking any alcohol and driving is illegal. Beware of driving with a hangover, because there will still be alcohol in your bloodstream.

Smoke is inescapable, and although the government recently banned smoking in public places, this is often ignored. Foreign cigarettes are a convenient bargaining tool in remote poorer areas.

Out and About

Bathrooms are often marked "Femei" for women and "Barbate" for men.

Violent crime is low relative to the rest of Europe, but petty crime is widespread. The most common is pickpocketing, money-changing scams, and con artists posing as "tourist police." (There is no such thing. Say no and walk away; otherwise, they will ask for money or to see your passport.)

Only use taxis with the approved taxi sign. Arrange the fee before you begin your journey.

There are a lot of stray dogs in Bucharest. Don't approach them, and keep well away from any packs.

Dress

Smart, casual clothing is adequate for most situations outside of business, although you should dress up more to go to the theater or a restaurant.

Gifts and Tips

It is customary to bring a small gift when visiting someone's home—an odd number of flowers, chocolates, or a bottle of wine.

You should tip 10 percent in restaurants for good service.

Russia

Meeting and Greeting

Greet with a firm handshake and give several quick shakes while maintaining good eye contact. You should shake hands like this even when meeting the same person every day; a simple hello is not sufficient. Men and women can also shake hands, although good friends and relatives embrace and kiss each other on the cheeks.

During social functions, wait to be introduced, rather than walking up to strangers and introducing yourself. Russians are not comfortable talking to strangers. You shouldn't say hello to people on the street or shopkeepers. In general, people don't make eye contact; they walk with their heads down and mind their own business. Old Communist habits are hard to break; Russians are still wary about whom they talk to, but once you get to know them they are very friendly and relaxed.

Punctuality is very flexible; expect to be kept waiting before a meeting.

Don't use first names until you are invited to do so. Russians often introduce themselves by stating just their surname.

Conversation
Russians love children, so make a fuss over them. Showing a photograph of your own family is a great way to break the ice.

Russians have spent many decades being very guarded about what they say, so they are used to the subtle nuances of language and may read subtext into what you are saying. However, directness is also much appreciated. Just be yourself and show respect to your hosts.

Eating and Drinking
Don't point out the relative poverty or sparse living conditions of Russian people. Many survive on less than $200 a month and work two jobs just to make ends meet. Russians can be very critical of their own country, but you should refrain from joining in. Despite this,

Russian hospitality is legendary, and they will take great care to entertain you in style, even if it means making financial sacrifices.

You will always be offered seconds on food, and you may have to leave a small amount uneaten to show that you are full. Otherwise, don't waste food, and eat what you are offered. Russians hate wasting food, money, or vodka.

Drinking vodka is inescapable, and a refusal is unacceptable unless you give a really good excuse (such as a medical or religious excuse). Otherwise, you will be expected to down shots of vodka in a single gulp. Don't forget to toast with every new glass (especially the host). If you turn up late to a Russian party, you may be expected to drink a good-natured forfeit shot of vodka (*shtrafnaya*).

Smoking is common, even during a meal. Non-smoking sections in restaurants are a rarity.

If you are a guest, the male host will usually pay, although it is polite to make a token offer to settle the bill if you are a man as well. A woman should never offer to pay the bill.

Water quality varies considerably in Russia. For peace of mind, use bottled water for drinking and brushing your teeth. Avoid ice, salads, and raw vegetables.

Out and About
The stereotype of the gloomy Russian can sometimes be true. You may not see many

smiles on the street, but behind closed doors, away from the dirty streets and staircases and once the vodka starts flowing at a party, things can get quite wild. A Russian home is a refuge, a place of sanctuary where the outside world is forgotten and people can be themselves.

Avoid Russian police. Many of them are corrupt and view tourists as mobile ATM machines. Carry your passport with you (or a photocopy for extra security). If you travel around the country, you must report to the local passport control office wherever you are staying.

There is a dual price system at many public attractions, such as museums, so expect to pay up to 10 times more than a Russian citizen for admission.

Russians often use hand gestures. One that might cause you confusion is when someone waves a hand across their throat in a gesture that in the West might suggest, "You're dead meat." In fact, in Russia it means "Stop" or "I'm full" or "I've had enough of this." Another Russian gesture involves tapping the neck with an index finger, which can mean that someone is drunk or drinks too much. It also may be an invitation to drink, much like the Western habit of mimicking raising an imaginary glass to your lips.

Don't whistle indoors; it brings bad luck or financial loss.

Lining up is not a thing of the past. For example, you may have to stand in line for a long time for a train ticket because everyone has to present his or her passport, even for internal travel.

Dress

Summers in Moscow are akin to those in northern Europe, but summer evenings can be cold. Russian winters are very cold outside, but temperatures inside are very warm, so dress in layers and bring well-insulated boots with good grips for the snow and ice. That is another reason why people walk bent over with their heads down in Russia—they are trying to stay on their feet.

Always remove your shoes when visiting a Russian home. Often you will be provided with guest slippers.

Gifts and Tips

Gift-giving is popular and appreciated, and gifts are opened immediately. Alcohol (other than vodka) is welcome, or a food item that is rare and expensive in Russia. Bring flowers for the woman of the house when visiting a home.

Tipping used to be illegal, but now a 10 percent service charge is usually added to the bill, and you may add another tip for excellent service. Don't scrutinize the bill—it indicates a lack of trust.

Saudi Arabia

Meeting and Greeting

Men should greet every other man in the room with a handshake and the words "Assalaam Alaikum" ("May peace be upon you"), to which he will reply "Waalaikum Assalaam" ("And peace also upon you"). Women should take their lead from the man, who may or may not shake hands depending on how Westernized he is. Greet the most senior person first, then greet around the room in a counterclockwise direction.

Close friends of the same sex may embrace. Women greet each other with a handshake or hug. Men should not greet or touch women unless they are blood relatives.

Conversation

Saudis, like most Arabs, are masters of small talk. In business there are always several minutes of pleasantries before discussions begin, and even then it will take several meetings to establish trust and build a relationship before business is discussed properly. Meetings are nearly always interrupted by phone calls and unexpected visitors, even family.

Don't change the subject of the conversation unless you are invited to do so. If you join in the middle of a discussion, your host will explain the subject and invite your contribution. You will gain respect for expressing your views honestly (especially concerning religion and politics), as long as your case is well reasoned. It doesn't matter if your opinion differs from that of others, since intelligent argument is a good way of demonstrating your intellect and provoking thought in a courteous and dignified way. A debate is a way of learning something from and about each other. This is very different from arguing, which should be avoided at all costs.

It is acceptable to inquire after a man's "family and children," but not his "wife and daughters." The only topic of discussion that is out of bounds is women, although you should also avoid hyperbole.

Saudis will always be polite, even if they don't like you. If you are ever treated in a less than polite way, it is a sign that your hosts feel comfortable enough with you to relax the customary protocol of impeccable manners. Take it as a compliment. Lavish hospitality isn't always a sign that a relationship is going well. Sometimes, in business, the most elaborate hospitality precedes a disappointment. Also, remember that yes can mean maybe, since Saudis like to let others down gently.

Eating and Drinking

Eat and pass plates of food with your right hand; the left hand is reserved for unclean uses such as going to the bathroom. Don't touch anyone with your left hand.

If someone offers you food or drink it is impolite to refuse, but you should not finish everything on your plate because this implies that the quantity of food was insufficient.

Serving coffee to visitors is an important Bedouin ritual called *gawha*, which involves roasting and then grinding the beans while your guests listen to the "music" of your labors with the pestle and mortar. The coffee is served with fresh dates. If coffee is served a second time, it may be a polite way of suggesting that it is time for you to leave.

Alcohol and pork are forbidden, even to visitors. A few embassies and business compounds have special dispensation, but otherwise there are very strict penalties for breaking the law.

Out and About

Try to observe correct etiquette, since Saudis are too polite to point out your social gaffes (with the exception of severe breaches of the law or morality).

It is okay to sit with your legs crossed as long as you don't point the soles of your feet at anyone.

Women never travel alone and are not allowed to drive; this applies to visitors. Driving is very dangerous, and despite the absence of alcohol, Saudis have one of the highest road fatality rates in the world. There is very little order: Cars frequently skip traffic lights, drivers rarely stay in lanes, and speed limits are often ignored.

Always ask permission before taking someone's photograph, and don't take pictures of women or government buildings.

Saudi males often walk hand in hand as a sign of friendship.

Speak in a calm and composed manner at all times. Raising your voice, gesturing, or becoming too animated is impolite.

Carry your *igama* (identification papers) everywhere.

Dress
Saudi women wear a black silk cloak called the *abaya*, along with a headscarf and veil. Saudi men wear a gown called a *thobe*. This is usually white, although during cool weather you will often see darker colors. Long black cloaks called *bisht* or *mishlah* often are worn over the *thobe*. The headdress consists of a large square of cloth (*ghutra*) folded into a triangle and held in place by a small white cap (*taiga*) and a black cord (*iqal*).

Visitors should dress modestly. Men should cover everything from their navels to their knees (so short-sleeved shirts are okay, but short pants are not). Female visitors usually wear the *abaya* over their clothing, but anything is acceptable as long as it covers the shoulders, arms to the wrist and knees. Headscarves are not essential, but they show respect for the culture. In the capital, Riyadh, dress requirements are stricter than in other cities because it is setting an example, so a headscarf is advisable. The *Mutawwa* (religious police with the daunting title "Commission for the Promotion of Virtue and Prevention of Vice") stop anyone who is dressed or behaving inappropriately.

Gifts and Tips
You should only give a gift to a very close friend; otherwise, your overfamiliarity will be viewed as a big insult. Gifts should be of the highest quality. Don't give jewelry or silk items to men; such items are considered effeminate. The recipient will show his respect and gratitude for a gift by carefully examining the item, so make sure it is worthy of such close scrutiny.

In a restaurant or hotel, a service charge is usually added to the bill, but you should tip an additional 10 percent for excellent service.

Singapore

Meeting and Greeting

Singaporean culture combines vibrant Western consumerism with uniquely Asian customs and etiquette. The population of nearly four million is made up of three-quarters Chinese, 14 percent Malays, and nearly eight percent Indians.

Punctuality is very important in business, but it is rude to arrive on time for social events (it is perceived as greedy). The guest of honor arrives last.

Third-party introductions are the norm, so wait to be introduced. Greet with a light handshake, which is usually softer and longer than a handshake in the West. (The handshake should be up to 10 seconds.)

Offer a business card with both hands, with the text facing away from you. When receiving a business card, it is polite to scrutinize it closely and then keep hold of it, rather than stuff it into your pocket (which is rude and also signifies the end of the meeting).

Conversation

Saying no is hard for a Singaporean, who will prefer to say something like "perhaps" or "I'll think about it" in order to be polite. Expect to be let down very gently.

Saving face is paramount in this culture, so you should never do or say anything likely to cause embarrassment—for example, expressing negative emotions, such as anger or irritation, or raising your voice. Western-style assertiveness and directness are rude. You should be understated and diplomatic at all times, especially about your achievements. Try to be accommodating and flexible; if you express disagreement with someone who doesn't know you well, you will be viewed as pushy, or even hostile and aggressive.

Eating and Drinking

If someone puts food on your plate, accept it as a sign of hospitality; it is rude to refuse, and you must sample a little of everything you are offered. However, since there is a greater range of food restrictions here than in the West (no pork for Muslim Malays; no meat for Hindu Indians), do not reciprocate, since the

other person might feel obliged to eat it out of politeness.

Use the thick end of your chopsticks when taking food from a communal dish. Don't dig around in a bowl looking for the best bits of food.

Always make a point of complimenting the host on the enjoyable food (even if it was not to your taste). Singaporeans go to ridiculous lengths to ensure that their hospitality runs smoothly, so you should acknowledge their attention to detail.

In hawker centers (similar to an American food court), the food is rated A, B, C, or D, which is the Ministry of Health and Environment grade of quality. Avoid anything labeled with a D.

Smoking is banned in public areas, lines, and public transportation, although you are allowed to smoke in air-conditioned karaoke bars, pubs, and discos. Fines are steep ($1,000 SGD for a first offense).

Chewing gum is illegal, and you are not even allowed to bring it into the country, so check your pockets before you arrive.

Out and About

Singapore has one of the lowest crime rates in the world, and penalties are charged for a wide range of misdemeanors. For example, jaywalking, failure to flush a toilet, spitting, or littering will cost you $1,000 SGD for a first offense.

Do not use your left hand when interacting socially with Indians or Malays; it is reserved for unclean uses such as going to the bathroom. Use your right hand to eat, pass food, gesture, and handle gifts.

When pointing, use your knuckle rather than an extended finger.

Don't kick, move, point at, or touch anything with your feet—they are unclean.

Avoid standing with your hands on your hips; this is an aggressive gesture.

Although lining up is not popular in China, it is very important in Singapore; cutting in line is considered very rude.

Dress

The heavy consumer culture is reflected in the dress, since status, rank, and wealth are highly valued (especially among the young business set). In business, because of the hot and humid climate, jackets are only worn at important meetings; a long-sleeved shirt and tie are acceptable at all other times. Women wear light suits and modest accessories and makeup. Above all, clean and dry is very important.

Remove your shoes when entering a Singaporean home.

Gifts and Tips

In business, gift-giving is important, but gifts should be presented to the whole group because individual achievement is secondary to the collective effort. Open gifts in private to avoid embarrassment. Government employees are not allowed to accept gifts (to avoid accusations of corruption). Expect the receiver to politely refuse the gift before accepting it.

In a restaurant, tipping is uncommon, though appreciated. (A 10 percent service charge is often added to the bill.) Don't hand a tip directly to the waiter or leave money on the table; when settling the bill, tell the waiter to keep the change.

South Africa

Meeting and Greeting

Introductions usually take place in order of seniority. Greet everyone in the room with a firm handshake and maintain good eye contact. The "African handshake," which involves slipping a free hand around the other person's thumb, is used between blacks and whites and between blacks, but not between whites.

Black South Africans are informal and leisurely in their greetings and may ask questions about your trip and your family. If a person supports his arm as he shakes your hand, he is acknowledging your superior social position.

Although the people may seem relaxed and laid-back, South African culture includes strong formality and is very courtesy-conscious. For example, men stand up when a woman or a senior enters the room.

South Africans are generally gregarious and chatty. If there is an awkward silence, then something is seriously wrong!

The pace of business is relatively slow. Being overly aggressive about deadlines or the pace of decision-making will be counterproductive. Being pushy in South Africa does not get things done; it just annoys people and loses you trust.

Exchanging business cards is normally done at the start of a meeting.

Conversation
Avoid the old official governmental terms—Bantu and "native"—when referring to black people. The expression "ethnic group" is preferable to "tribe."

Racism is still a big problem, but if you treat everyone with respect you should encounter few difficulties.

Eating and Drinking

Eating customs and menus are similar to those in Western Europe, although in rural areas there may be ethnic differences. In some places a spoon or fingers are used to eat. Eating on the street is rare.

If you're invited to a South African home for dinner, your family is usually included in the invitation.

Out and About

Don't point at someone with your index finger wagging; it will be interpreted as a personal challenge.

Talking with your hands in your pockets is considered rude.

It is customary for African men to precede women when passing through a doorway.

Maintain a calm and quiet voice in conversations and meetings. Raising your voice is insulting and challenging.

It is normal for people of the same sex to walk hand in hand as a sign of friendship.

You will often hear the expressions "now-now" and "just now." The former means "immediately"; the latter means "later."

Dress

When dining out or in someone's home, a man should wear a jacket and tie.

For women, skirts and dresses are the norm, although this is changing slowly. Scarves are popular accessories. In rural communities, women should avoid wearing sleeveless, low-cut, or otherwise revealing clothes.

Tennis shoes are still items of sportswear, not daily attire.

Gifts and Tips

Always arrive at a dinner party with a gift. Expensive gifts aren't necessary, but flowers, chocolates, or a good bottle of wine are popular choices.

Waiters earn low wages, so tip at least 10 percent of the bill, unless the service is poor.

Spain

Meeting and Greeting

In business, initial greetings are formal, with handshakes and direct eye contact while saying "Buenos días/tardes/noches" for "Good morning/afternoon/evening or night." Shaking hands upon departure is popular, though not essential.

Socially, male friends often enjoy an *abrazo* (a bear hug with much backslapping), while women usually kiss men and women on both cheeks.

Personal space is small. Spaniards like to get up close and make frequent physical contact (pats and slaps), so don't back away; they will think you are being shy and quickly close the gap again. Or, worse, they will think you are being unfriendly.

Spain has one of the most flexible attitudes toward time in the world. Trains and buses seem to write their own timetables, and it is common to arrive half an hour late for social events. Spanish bureaucracy—in fact, anything involving documentation—is always infuriatingly prolonged. However, if you want to enjoy your visit, go with the flow rather than fighting this slow pace of life, because you'll never change it.

Conversation

The Spanish are gregarious, lively, and immediately friendly. They place much importance on personal and family relationships, so trust and respect, especially in business, are built up by your ability to interact with and enjoy the company of others, not by your credentials or qualifications. Spaniards tend to downplay their achievements and dislike those who try too hard or show off.

Conversation is often loud and very animated, with numerous hand gestures that a visitor might mistakenly interpret as signs of anger. Good-natured banter is okay as long as you don't insult Spanish culture or highlight racial stereotypes.

Familiarize yourself with the concept of *mañana*, which means "tomorrow" and is a habitual response to questions that require a definite answer. If you want to know when your car will be fixed, it will always be *mañana*. This can seem like laziness, but actually Spaniards never like to be seen as trying too hard.

Eating and Drinking

When dining out in the evening, Spaniards socialize and eat late, and they bring their children with them. It is not uncommon to book a table for 10 p.m., and many of the bars and clubs don't liven up until midnight.

For formal meals, the host and hostess sit at opposite ends of the table, with the guests of honor of the opposite sex placed to their right.

To make a toast, raise your glass and say "Salud."

Clear your plate; leaving food is considered wasteful.

Out and About
Public displays of affection are very common and acceptable among the younger generation, but much like in other European countries, you rarely see older people being overtly affectionate in public.

To beckon someone in Spain, extend your arm with your palm downward and wriggle your fingers toward yourself.

Smoking is widespread, and it is difficult to escape the smoke wherever there are groups of people around, even at the dinner table.

If you need to use the bathroom, it is acceptable to use the facilities in a cafe or bar without buying a drink. The men's room is labeled "Caballeros" and the women's room is labeled "Señoras."

Yawning or stretching in public is rude.

Spaniards love taking walks, and there is a tradition of taking a stroll (*paseo*) before dinner. The streets are full of people of all ages casually working up an appetite.

Dress
Older women wear dresses, but younger women also wear pants, although jeans are not as ubiquitous as in the United States and other parts of Europe. Leather clothes and accessories are very popular. Only tourists wear shorts or sweatpants. Designer brand names and high-quality elegant clothing are appreciated.

The *mantilla* is a traditional black lightweight lace or silk scarf worn over the head and shoulders by older Spanish women on special occasions, along with a rigid headpiece called a *peineta*.

Gifts and Tips
Gifts are always opened in front of the giver. If you are invited to a Spanish home, bring a small gift, such as chocolates or flowers.

Restaurant bills include a service charge by law, but you may leave an extra tip of between 5 and 10 percent for excellent service.

Sweden

Meeting and Greeting

Punctuality is very important. You must arrive on time, not even five minutes early and certainly not late. A social invitation for 8 p.m. means just that—the food may already be on the table. If you are going to be late, call the host ahead to warn and apologize.

Greet with a firm handshake (with men and women) while maintaining good eye contact, and say "God dag" ("Good day"). Shake hands again upon departure. "Hello" is "Hej" (pronounced *hay*) and "Goodbye" is "Hej då" (pronounced *hay door*). When entering a shop or restaurant, you should acknowledge every-one (except customers) with a "Hej."

Conversation

Swedes say "Tack" ("Thank you") a lot. If you want to say "Thank you very much," say "Tack tack" or "Tack så mycket" (pronounced *tack so moo ka*).

Keep hand gestures to a minimum. The Swedes use few gestures when speaking and are not comfortable with a lot of bodily contact, so maintain an arm's length of personal space and avoid backslapping and other overt physical expressions. Speak in a calm and composed manner at all times. You rarely hear people raising their voices in Sweden.

Show respect to older people, who can be quite formal.

Swedes are Scandinavian, but they aren't Norwegians or Danes, so don't offend people by lumping them together or confusing them with these other nationalities.

Always be direct and honest. Avoid hyperbole, and do not make idle promises or invitations. If a Swede says yes, you can be certain that he means it. He will only say it when he is sure that he can mean it, to avoid unfilled expectations.

Eating and Drinking

The smorgasbord originated in Sweden. It is polite to try a little of everything (although if cold herring turns your stomach, no one will be offended if you pass), starting with *sill* (herring in a variety of sauces), boiled potatoes and sour cream, followed by cold cuts, hot food (often more fish), and then cheese, dessert, and coffee.

At formal dinner parties, the male guest of honor sits to the left of the hostess and the female guest of honor sits to the right of the host. There may even be a seating plan.

To make a toast, say "Skål," then look everyone in the eye, take a drink, and then make eye contact again before putting down the glass. Don't make a toast or start drinking until the host has made a toast.

When shopping for groceries, it is customary to buy what you touch.

If you see a Swede with a small lump under his top lip, he's using Snus, a moist ground tobacco product dating from the late 1700s, which is more popular than smoking. (It's actually regulated as a foodstuff.) At a party, cigarette smokers often gather underneath the kitchen fan, since it's better than going outside into the cold.

Out and About
Anywhere in the countryside that isn't fenced off is *Allemansrätten*, meaning "right for everyone" to walk or camp. However, you must leave the place as you found it and respect the land.

Manhole covers in Sweden are labeled with different letters. The most common is A, which stands for "Avbruten kärlek" ("lost love"), whereas K stands for "Kärlek" ("love"). It's a fun superstition to step on or avoid manhole covers depending on what fortune they bring.

Always remove your shoes before entering a Swedish home.

It is illegal to spank children. Consequently, Swedes are very skilled at disciplining their children using reasoning and understanding. They don't just obey the law; they firmly believe that spanking is wrong.

Dress
Swedes dress well and fashionably without being ostentatious, although business dress is often quite relaxed. Clothes are not used to demonstrate status or wealth. Everyone dresses well but more or less the same, in keeping with the egalitarian ethics of the culture.

Gifts and Tips
It is customary to bring a small gift when you are visiting someone's home. Alcohol is very expensive, so a vintage whiskey or other spirit is always welcome.

A service charge is often included in the bill, but you should leave another 10 percent for excellent service.

Switzerland

Meeting and Greeting

Switzerland combines French, Italian, and German speakers, so the greetings may differ accordingly, but a widespread gesture given on arrival and departure is a firm handshake with good eye contact (with children as well as adults). If you are kissed on the cheek you will usually receive three kisses. It is safest to use a handshake and only kiss when the other person initiates it. Introductions are usually made by a third party.

For "Hello," the German speakers say "Grüß Gott" (or "God's Greeting," as in Austria) or "Grüezi" rather than "Guten tag" ("Good day"). The French say "Bonjour," and the Italians say, "Buon giorno" (both meaning "good day").

Conversation

Initially the Swiss can seem quite formal and polite, but the interaction will relax after you become more familiar. The status quo usually prevails, so making new friends is not a major priority, but they are honest and straightforward, if conservative. Respect the privacy of others, and do not ask personal questions about age, politics, income, or religious beliefs.

The Swiss are very well-behaved and are sticklers for doing things the right way and obeying the rules. But they are also very direct and dislike fake honesty for the sake of keeping up appearances. They will take what you say very literally, so idle promises or invitations, such as "We must do this again sometime," will be taken at face value. They are also very good listeners. If someone is talking, don't interrupt. Always wait until the other person has finished speaking.

Don't keep smiling, making jokes, and being overly friendly too soon; you will gain more trust and respect if you are restrained and dignified at first. Friendship is built slowly; overfamiliarity is considered superficial and viewed with distrust.

Eating and Drinking
In many cultures it is polite to begin eating only when everyone else has been served. In Switzerland this extends to drinking as well. When toasting, make eye contact with everyone in a group individually before you take a sip.

Out and About
Maintain good posture—no slouching or relaxed poses. Do not put your hands in your pockets. Always say hello to everyone (customers included) when you enter shops, especially small ones.

The Swiss will wait at a traffic light even when there are no cars in sight, and they never jaywalk.

Littering will not be tolerated. If you drop so much as a candy wrapper, you are likely to be told off by a member of the public. Switzerland is clean and litter-free (and the public toilets are immaculate)—the Swiss want to keep it that way.

Dress
The Swiss are smart dressers who believe in presenting a clean and elegant image. Good taste and modesty are valued above showiness and ostentatious displays of wealth. Wear jewelry and accessories that are simple and understated.

Gifts and Tips
If you are invited to dinner at a Swiss home, arrive on time and bring some flowers or a modest gift for the hostess. Anything too expensive is showy and may cause embarrassment.

A service charge of 15 percent is included in the bill by law, but it is common practice to round up.

Taiwan

Meeting and Greeting

The Taiwanese bow or nod their heads, often without smiling, because greeting is a solemn, respectful affair. Keep eye contact brief. If you do shake hands, the shake will be limp and longer than in the West; this does not imply a lack of assertiveness. Rather, a firm handshake may be interpreted as pushy and aggressive. Women rarely shake hands. Introductions are by a third person.

Resist the urge to ask everyone to use your first name immediately; trust and respect are built slowly, so rushing the relationship will result in embarrassment and confusion.

Offer a business card with both hands, with the text facing away from you. When receiving a business card, it is polite to scrutinize it closely and then place it on the table, rather than stuffing it into your pocket (which is rude and also signifies the end of the meeting).

Conversation

In China, you should avoid talking about Taiwan (and don't refer to it as a separate country). Here, you should refer to the "Taiwan Province" or just "Taiwan." Although the 25 percent of inhabitants who came over from China after World War II may still consider themselves politically Chinese, the remainder very much consider themselves Taiwanese (even though culturally they are Chinese).

Always deny a compliment graciously (don't say "Thank you"); it is important to show modesty. Expect to be asked very personal questions, even by complete strangers, such as "How much do you earn?" or "Are you married?" that should be deflected tactfully, if you wish to keep these things private.

In the West, it is customary to discuss a wide range of subjects while eating; in Taiwan, the conversation revolves around the food, almost obsessively, with endless compliments to the host.

Eating and Drinking

When eating, sample a little of everything and leave a little food on your plate at the end of the meal; otherwise, your host will think you are still hungry. If someone puts food on your plate, accept this offer of hospitality and eat at least some of it. Be sure you compliment the food several times.

Expect frequent toasting. The host utters the first toast with the words "Gan bei," or "dry the glass," after which everyone should drain their glasses.

Use the thick end of your chopsticks (or the larger serving chopsticks) when taking food from a communal dish. Take the food closest to you and don't dig around in a bowl looking for the best morsels.

Eat rice by holding the bowl close to your face and scooping the rice into your mouth with your chopsticks. Leaving the bowl on the table is a sign that you are unhappy with the food. Never leave your chopsticks stuck in your rice; this is associated with death.

When the bill arrives, it is customary for everyone to fight to pay it. If you are hosting, you should pay, so the best way to avoid a battle at the end of the meal is to settle the bill discreetly in private.

Out and About
Driving in Taiwan is chaotic. There are lots of scooters, and many drive on the wrong side of the road. (Be careful when turning a corner.) Also, some people drive with their headlights off to save gas! It is not unusual to see five people crammed onto one scooter. If you are involved in an accident, the other party may try to offer you money to avoid involving the police.

When the Taiwanese aren't eating, they love shooting off fireworks, no matter what the occasion. Expect to hear loud bangs every day. Earthquakes and tremors occur very frequently here, too (every week); it is a fact of life and people are used to it.

Just because people don't smile or acknowledge others on the street, it doesn't mean that they are miserable or rude. As a foreigner, you will attract a lot of friendly curiosity and lots of stares; don't get annoyed, or you'll soon draw a large crowd with your inappropriate behavior! Remain calm at all times.

Saying no is hard for a Taiwanese person, who will prefer to say something such as "perhaps" or "I'll think about it" in order to be polite. Try to understand the subtext of any exchange, since the Taiwanese are very diplomatic and will go out of their way to save face. If you need to discuss a sensitive subject, do so in private so you don't embarrass someone in public. Causing someone to lose face would be a disaster not only for your relationship, but for their whole family.

Dress
Dress in neat, clean clothes; avoid clothing that makes you stand out. (You'll get enough unwarranted attention without making your appearance even more unusual.) Take off your shoes when entering a private home.

Gifts and Tips
Taiwanese people will politely decline a gift three times before accepting it. They will not open it in front of you, nor should you. Accept a gift with two hands, with your palms facing upward.

Foreign cigarettes, wine, and spirits make good presents, but don't bring food to a dinner party because it implies that the hospitality is insufficient. Wrap gifts in paper with lucky colors, such as red, yellow, or pink—not black or white, which are associated with death.

Tipping is increasingly common. Many restaurants add a 10 percent service charge. Add another 10 percent for good service.

Thailand

Meeting and Greeting

Thais do not shake hands; they greet each other with a *wai*. Place your hands together as if in prayer and raise them to your face while bowing slightly. The height of your hands depends on the status of the other person. When you *wai* an equal, the hands are placed on the chest; for monks and elders they are raised to nose- or forehead-level; Buddha should be *waied* with your hands above your head. Don't *wai* children or people who are serving you, such as waiters, hotel staff, and taxi drivers, just nod slightly. Foreigners should not initiate a *wai*.

For "Hello," men say "Sawatdee krup" and women say "Sawatdee kaa."

Conversation

Patience, tolerance, and calmness are highly prized virtues. Losing your temper, raising your voice, or attempting to dominate others physically or verbally is totally inappropriate—it will lose you all respect and is totally counterproductive. Always stay cool and polite, regardless of the circumstances.

Thai people are very sensitive, so even a misjudged joke could damage your relationship or cause embarrassment. If you feel that you might have committed a breach of etiquette, no matter how minor, always apologize by offering a *wai*.

Eating and Drinking

Thais eat with a fork and spoon. Food is bite-sized, so a knife is unnecessary. Only the spoon should enter your mouth, while the fork is used to push food onto the spoon. When picking up food (such as sticky rice), always use your right hand. Do not lick your fingers.

Groups of Buddhist monks walk through the streets each morning carrying bowls to receive offers of food. It is an honor to give food to monks, so you should thank them, not vice versa.

Out and About

Never criticize members of the Thai royal family, even in jest. Any disrespect shown toward them (and the currency upon which their faces appear) can attract a charge of *lèse majesté*, which carries severe punishment. When the national anthem is played daily at 8 a.m. and 6 p.m., you should stand in respectful silence. Take your lead from those around you.

It is also an offense to insult or disrespect any religion (not just Buddhism); this includes behaving inappropriately toward religious images or when visiting temples.

All images of Buddha are considered sacred. Do not touch, point your feet toward, stand higher than, turn your back on, or pose for photographs in front of a Buddha. Remove your shoes before entering a room that contains a Buddha.

Monks are not allowed to touch or be touched by women. If a woman wants to pass something to a monk, she should place it on a piece of cloth and step away.

Never touch a Thai person on the head, even a child. Symbolically (and literally), it is the highest part of the body. If you touch a person's head, even by accident, apologize immediately. The feet, as the lowest part, should never touch or be pointed toward anybody. When sitting on a chair, keep the soles of your feet on the floor; when sitting on the floor, cross your legs, tucking your feet underneath and to the side so they don't point at anyone. Never sit with your legs straight out in front of you.

Public displays of affection should not go beyond holding hands. Hugging a Thai person or kissing in public, even as a gesture of friendship, is unwelcome.

Smiling is often used to disguise negative emotions such as anger, embarrassment, or disapproval; it is not always a sign of amusement.

Buddhists believe that all life is sacred, so accidentally stepping on a spider or an insect is regrettable; deliberately swatting or squashing one will cause great offense.

Dress

Even on the beach, Thai people do not strip down to bikinis and shorts. They are prepared to tolerate tourists wearing them on the beach, but elsewhere you should cover up your legs and arms (especially in temples, where men should wear hats and women should wear scarves and collars buttoned to the neck). Going topless or nude anywhere is disrespectful (and illegal). Clothes should be clean and dry. Showering regularly is important; nobody will criticize you for doing it four times a day.

Remove your shoes before entering a Thai home; even some offices and shops will expect you to leave your shoes at the door. Shoes are allowed in a temple compound, but not in the main chapel. Do not step on the threshold as you enter a room.

When you are hanging lower-body clothing to dry (such as pants, underwear, socks, etc.), they should be hung lower and well away from clothes worn on the upper body.

Gifts and Tips

Either give a gift with your right hand, with your left hand holding your right elbow, or use both hands. Before receiving a gift, it is usual to perform a *wai*.

Turkey

Close friends of either sex may use a two-handed handshake and a kiss on each cheek. It is customary when greeting elders to kiss their hand and touch it to your forehead. You should always stand up when an elder enters the room.

Traditionally, the titles *Bey* (for men) or *Hanim* (for women) are used after the first name, although a more modern form of address uses *Bay* (for men) or *Bayan* (for women) before the surname.

Conversation

Turks are very hospitable, and strangers will frequently invite you into their homes to share a cup of tea or coffee or a meal.

Turkish men are not supposed to talk to married women outside of their own family, and girls and married women should only talk to male family members. For example, if a Western couple stopped a Turkish man and the woman asked for directions, the Turk may ignore the woman, but be very helpful and friendly toward the man.

Meeting and Greeting

Upon arrival, greet everyone in the room in descending order of age, with a firm handshake and direct eye contact, and say "Merhaba" ("Hello") and "Nasilsiniz?" ("How are you?"). The usual response will be "Elyiyim teshekur ederim" ("Fine, thank you"). Handshakes are not necessary upon departure.

Eating and Drinking

In a restaurant, Turks generally order one course at a time, and service is very fast. The host will always pay the bill.

Smoking is very popular, especially between meal courses. You will also see people everywhere smoking water pipes called *narguileh*.

Turkish tea is drunk everywhere in small, tapered glasses with sugar, but without milk. Coffee is strong, with or without milk, and often quite sweet, unless you ask for it without sugar.

During Ramazan (Turkish for Ramadan), you shouldn't eat, drink, or smoke in the presence of locals until after sunset.

Out and About

On public transportation, women should not sit next to male strangers. Women also are not allowed in a traditional tea or coffee house.

Don't blow your nose in public, especially in restaurants.

It is normal for people of the same sex to walk hand in hand as a sign of friendship.

Carry identification with you at all times—it is required by law.

Remove your shoes if you are invited into a Turkish home, and don't show the soles of your feet to anyone. (Sit with your feet flat on the floor.)

Shaking your head means "I don't understand"; it doesn't mean no. If you shake your head, people might repeat what they have just said. To say no, raise your eyebrows and make a "tsk" sound, or tilt your head backward slightly. Nod your head to say yes.

Attract attention by waving your hand up and down, rather than side to side.

Turkey is one of the most moderate Islamic countries in the world, but you should still avoid public displays of affection with members of the opposite sex, including hugging someone to say hello.

Don't cross your arms while facing someone; it is considered rude.

Foreign visitors are allowed to visit any mosque, but you should cover up and avoid prayer times. Photography is allowed anywhere, apart from at military and police installations.

Dress

Business dress is conservative, and female visitors should dress modestly, with high necklines and low hemlines. Head coverings are optional (although advisable in the heat).

Don't wear shorts unless you're at the beach.

Gifts and Tips

If you are invited to dinner at a Turkish home, bring some flowers or a modest gift for the hostess and any children. If you bring wine or spirits, check in advance to make sure your host drinks alcohol.

A service charge is not included in the bill, and it is normal to leave a 5 to 10 percent tip. Give money with your right hand. (The left hand is reserved for unclean uses, such as going to the bathroom.)

United Kingdom

Meeting and Greeting

On first meeting, greet with a firm handshake (men and women), while smiling and maintaining good eye contact, and say "How do you do?" or more generally, "Pleased to meet you." In less formal situations or with a large group of people, using the American group wave and saying "Hi" is okay. Outside of business it isn't customary to shake hands again when leaving.

Friends (not men) often kiss on one or two cheeks. Because there is no longer a norm, few people in the UK really know whether they should shake hands or how many cheeks to kiss, so introductions can sometimes be quite awkward.

Punctuality is important, but it is customary to arrive about 15 minutes late to a dinner party.

Conversation

In social events, you are expected to make small talk with those you have just met; favorite topics include the weather and your journey ("Have you come far?"), although any topic is acceptable as long as the conversation keeps flowing without uncomfortable pauses, and you are polite, smile, and show genuine interest in what other people have to say.

Overt displays of status and wealth are vulgar, but often subtle social markers seep into the conversation because people casually drop in details about their lifestyle to establish their place in the pecking order.

Asking someone "What do you do?" is considered rather clumsy, and the British tend to take a more indirect route to find out such information. For example, "Do you travel much for your work?" gives the other person the chance to reveal what he or she does for a living, should that person wish to slip it into the conversation.

In general, you will be judged more on your social confidence and how you present yourself than on what you say.

Eating and Drinking

Place your napkin on your lap; don't tuck it under your chin.

With many courses, start with the cutlery on the outside and work your way in. Keep your knife and fork in your right and left hands, respectively, at all times; don't put down your knife to eat with your fork in the United States style.

To make a toast, raise your glass as high as your head and say "Cheers." It isn't necessary to maintain eye contact while toasting. A toast is usually only said once, rather than repeated as is customary in eastern Europe.

In business, the host usually pays; otherwise, it is normal to split the bill unless someone has expressly taken you out for a treat. Even then you should make a show of wanting to make a contribution before you graciously accept.

Avoid smoking during a meal, and do not smoke in a nonsmoking area in a restaurant.

Out and About

Cutting in line is considered very rude. Sometimes Brits will be quietly indignant without actually confronting you about it, whereas other times, someone will curtly tell you to wait in line. It all depends on the size of the line (and the size of the people).

Public displays of affection are acceptable in moderation, but if a couple get too explicit, they are likely to be viewed with ridicule (rather than with any sense of moral outrage), since prolonged petting is considered adolescent and in poor taste.

Talking to strangers is more common in the north of the UK, but in the big cities (especially London) it is uncommon. Also, people rarely speak to strangers on the Tube (underground train system).

Dress

Business dress among senior managers is quite conservative, although in many companies a shirt and tie without a jacket is acceptable, as are a skirt or pants and a blouse for women (or even casual dress, depending on the corporate culture). It is not uncommon to see all these styles of dress in the same company, depending on status and which people are in contact with customers or other corporations.

Unlike many egalitarian European countries, where everyone dresses the same regardless of status, in the UK social standing and wealth greatly influence choice of clothing. In general, an upper-middle-class person would dress in smart casual clothing rather than a jogging suit, a football shirt, and designer tennis shoes, although everyone is free to express them- selves. You would have to wear something very outrageous to attract stares.

People dress up to go out in the evening, but this varies greatly depending on social status and corresponding choice of entertainment. For instance, in a cinema, practically any clothing is acceptable, whereas a first-class restaurant would expect diners to wear smart casual clothing or a jacket and tie.

In some homes you should remove your shoes (except during a dinner party); in others it doesn't matter. When in doubt, ask.

Gifts and Tips

Always bring a good bottle of wine to a dinner party. Flowers for the hostess are optional, although much appreciated.

A service charge is usually only added to the bill in very fancy restaurants. You should add 10 percent as long as the service was acceptable.

United States

Meeting and Greeting

The customary greeting is a firm handshake with good eye contact. Say "Hello" or "How are you?" This is not an inquiry into the state of your health, so just say "Hi" or "Hello" in reply if you are greeted in this manner. Family members and close friends may hug. Men rarely embrace each other or kiss cheeks. It is not necessary to shake hands upon leaving, except in business or to conclude a deal.

Use a person's title and last name until you are invited to use first names, which will invariably be immediately. This is not a sign of intimacy; Americans feel that the use of last names is so formal that it is uncomfortable to address others in this manner. You will find that Americans almost always introduce them-selves or others using first names, even in business. If you are introduced to someone by his or her first name, then it is perfectly acceptable to use the first name.

Punctuality is important in business. Always phone ahead if you are going to be more than 10 minutes late. Likewise, punctuality is valued for prestigious social engagements. However, punctuality is considerably more flexible for casual gatherings among friends; being a few minutes late is the norm, and it's not unheard of for people to trickle into a casual party among friends anywhere from 15 minutes to an hour after the designated starting time of the party.

Conversation

Americans are generally very gregarious and welcoming. Frequent smiling is a cultural norm, an important social custom that should not be misinterpreted as superficiality. Maintain a personal distance of at least one arm's length.

Conversation can be animated, quite loud, and refreshingly direct. Although in some situations political correctness obliges people to choose their words carefully so they won't offend anyone, in others you will meet some of the most straightforward people in the world. The freedom to express one's opinion is highly prized in the United States.

Many Americans strive to be upbeat and have a positive outlook in the belief that good things come to those who are prepared to work hard and put their faith in life, liberty, and the pursuit of happiness, three principles upon which the country was founded. The culture is very flexible and competitive, so excellence and achievement are highly valued, along with ambition, wealth, power, and fame. It is acceptable to discuss your achievements; many Americans believe that the rewards of capitalism are available to everyone, regard-less of their background.

If someone compliments you, accept it and say "Thank you." It is not necessary to deny the compliment or be self-effacing, as it is in some other cultures.

Eating and Drinking

Most Americans eat with the fork in the right hand and switch hands to pick up the knife for cutting or spreading. But the continental style of cutlery use (knife and fork remain in right and left hands, respectively) is also acceptable. It is normal to eat fast food with one's hands, or to pick up a burger, sandwich, or slice of pizza in a restaurant.

Portions are very large and food is generally cheap. It is okay to leave food on your plate because waste is rarely frowned upon in this consumer culture. Refusing food is also acceptable. Eating and drinking in public is commonplace.

In business the host usually pays; otherwise, it is normal to split the bill unless someone has expressly taken you out for a treat. Even then

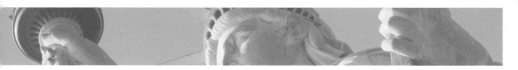

you should make a show of wanting to make a contribution before you graciously accept.

Attract a waiter's attention by gaining eye contact and raising your eyebrows. You can also raise your index finger after you catch your waiter's eye, but snapping your fingers is considered rude. If you mimic signing a check when the waiter is on the other side of the room, he will understand that you want him to bring the bill.

Smoking restrictions differ between states, and it is prohibited in many public places. It is polite to ask whether you can smoke; if people object they will say so. During a meal, don't smoke between courses.

If an invitation says "potluck" or "covered dish," it means bring a plate of food. That way, when everyone shares, there will be enough to go around. "B.Y.O.B." means "bring your own bottle."

At a dinner party, don't start eating until others have started or the host tells you to eat. In some households, a short prayer of thanks for the food will be said before the meal.

Out and About
Don't arrive unannounced at someone's house. Arrange a visit beforehand. It is customary for the host to show you around his home if it is your first visit.

Dress
Business dress varies depending on the corporate culture. Take your lead from those around you.

Outside of work, clean casual clothes, including jeans, T-shirts, shorts, and tennis shoes, are widely worn.

Gifts and Tips
When you are invited to someone's home, bring a small gift—a bottle of wine, candy, or flowers.

Tipping in restaurants is obligatory, and you are expected to tip at least 15 percent of the bill. Restaurant owners are not required by law to pay minimum wage to serving staff, so they rely on tips to make a living. In recent years, tipping closer to 20 percent is common if the service was good. Tipping less than 15 percent is considered rude.

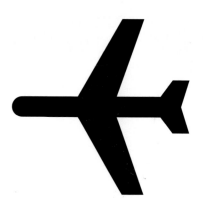